Henry Inman

Stories of the Old Santa Fe Trail

Henry Inman

Stories of the Old Santa Fe Trail

ISBN/EAN: 9783744725477

Printed in Europe, USA, Canada, Australia, Japan

Cover: Foto ©Andreas Hilbeck / pixelio.de

More available books at **www.hansebooks.com**

STORIES

OF THE

OLD SANTA FE TRAIL.

By COL. HENRY INMAN,
OF KANSAS.

KANSAS CITY, MO.:
BOOK PUBLISHING HOUSE OF RAMSEY, MILLETT & HUDSON.
1881.

TO CAPTAIN HENRY KING, OF TOPEKA, WHOSE PEN FIRST ELEVATED THE LITERATURE OF KANSAS TO THE DIGNITY OF THE "ATLANTIC" AND "SCRIBNER," AND TO HON. C. C. SPRIGG, OF ELLSWORTH, AND CAPTAIN HENRY BOOTH, OF LARNED, WHOSE FRIENDSHIP HAS BEEN OF THE NOBLEST AND MOST EXALTED CHARACTER, THESE SKETCHES ARE INSCRIBED.

AUTHOR'S NOTE.

The reader is reminded that the Atchison, Topeka & Santa Fe Railroad practically follows the old Santa Fe Trail, or wagon road, across the Plains, through Kansas and New Mexico. No other scope of country on the continent, perhaps, is so rich in history and tradition. The advent of the railroad, with its disturbing and disclosing influences, has made this land a new one to every day eyes; but, in fact, it was already old when the Pilgrims landed at Plymouth Rock. It is not possible, of course, in the brief space of such a book as this, to give a symmetrical or connected account of the many strange, stirring and important scenes enacted here in such a prolonged and confused period of time. The author has contented himself, therefore, with merely gathering up a few separate and characteristic fragments of its wonderful story, which it is hoped will interest the general reader, and stimulate further research in this vast field of shadow and mystery.

CONTENTS.

How Pawnee Rock was Named. (Illustrated.) 1
The March of Francisco Vasquez de Coronado . . . 11
The Legend of Tepeyacac 60
The Fight on Lowrey's Island Twenty Years Ago . 74
A Legend of Pawnee Rock 83
Another Legend of Pawnee Rock 94
A Terrible Ten Miles Ride. (Illustrated.) 110
The Massacre at Babb's Ranch 150
The Scouts' Last Ride 164
Wal Henderson 194
Cannady's Ranch 312
Gen'l Forsyth's Fight on the Arrickaree Fork. (Illustrated.) 251
A Lively Race with the Kiowas 269
Se-Quo-Yah 274
Will the Buffalo Become Extinct? 286

PAWNEE ROCK.

STORIES OF OLD SANTA FE TRAIL.

HOW "PAWNEE ROCK" WAS NAMED.

I have no doubt that many of my readers have heard of "Kit Carson," the famous scout, Indian fighter and brave "frontiersman;" and also, that they have heard of "Pawnee Rock" in the now great State of Kansas—perhaps some of them have ridden by this once celebrated battle-ground of the "Pawnees," on their way to the mountains over the Atchison, Topeka & Santa Fe Railroad. If they have, this story of how it got its name will be doubly interesting.

"Pawnee Rock" is located only a few miles from the thriving little town of Larned, and is a classic spot in the Indian history of the "Great Plains." Its rugged mass of brown sandstone throws a deep shadow almost immediately over the broad trail that for hundreds of years was the highway of all the "Prairie Tribes" on their periodical hunts to the feeding grounds of the buffalo—southward, across the Canadian, and to the north, far beyond the Platte. Under the gloom, too, of its craggy and rough-hewn face—not a hundred yards away—that great international roadway, now a mere memory, the "Santa Fe Trail" passed.

In early Fall, when the "Rock" is wrapped in the soft amber haze—a distinguishing characteristic of the delightful "Indian Summer" on the "Central Plains;" or in the nascent Spring, when the mirage weaves its mysterious and weird-like shape, it looms up in the landscape like a huge mountain, and to the inexperienced eye on the prairie, it appears as if it were the continuation of a well-defined range. But when the frost comes, and the mist is dispelled, and when the thin fringe of timber on the Walnut—a few miles away—has doffed its emerald mantle, and the grass has grown yellow and rusty, then in the golden sunlight of Winter the "Rock" sinks down to its natural proportions, and cuts the clear blue of the skies with sharply-marked lines.

If this giant sentinel of the "Plains" might speak, what a story it could tell of the events that have happened on the beautiful prairie stretching out for miles at its feet! All over its scarred and weather-beaten front, carved in quaint and rude letters, are the names of hundreds who in early days made the dangerous and exciting passage of the Santa Fe Trail. Some names are roughly chiseled there, too, who were not ambitious at the time of a more enduring fame, and gave no further thought to their effort than was concentrated in the bare idea of relief from the *ennui* of the moment, while their horses and mules were resting, but who will go down to history cursed or praised—as viewed from varying aspects—long after the storm of centuries shall have obliterated every mark on this isolated mass of sandstone. Conspicuous among these is that of Robert E. Lee, the famous leader of the Confederate armies, who, in 1843, crossed into the borders of Mexico as an officer of the "Mounted Rifles." Under the shadow of "Pawnee Rock," perhaps Coronado, the celebrated Spanish explorer, and his little band of faithful followers rested on their lonely march in search of the mythical Quivira. The "Rock" alone is all that remains, in all probability, upon which the Spaniards looked, for the mighty interval of nearly four hundred years, must have relegated all else—trees, water courses and the entire landscape, that the hardy adventurers looked upon, to the domain of vast modification—and this iron-bound hill—whose unsusceptibility to change is almost as the earth itself—the only witness of their famous march.

During the half century included between the years 1823-73—which latter date marked the advent of the railroad in this portion of Kansas—"Pawnee Rock" was considered the most dangerous place on all the "Central Plains" for encounters with the Indians, as at this particular point on the "Trail" the Pawnees, Kiowas, Comanches, Arrapahoes and Cheyennes made their not infrequent successful raids upon the pack and wagon trains of the freighters across the continent. I well remember, in the earlier geographies, that most exciting and sensational of all the illustrations—to my boyish mind at least—which depicted the "Santa Fe traders attacked by Indians;" but that was long ago, and such scenes have passed away forever.

In those primitive days of the "Border," "Kit Carson," "Lucien B. Maxwell," "Old John Smith," the Bents and the Boones, with other famous frontiersmen, commenced their eventful lives in the "Far West"—mere boys then—but whose exploits have since made for them a world-wide reputation. "Kit Carson," "Maxwell," "Smith" and the Bents are dead—died with harness on, and on the confines of that civilization which is rapidly closing up the gap at the foot of the mountains, amidst which there would soon have been nothing congenial—so they passed away while there still remained fresh prairies and quiet streams.

"Kit," one of the most noble men it has been my fortune to know, is sleeping peacefully under the gnarled old Cottonwoods at Fort Lyon, on the Arkansas—that river he loved so well—every foot of whose silent margin could tell a story of his daring. It was at "Pawnee Rock," many, many years ago, that "Kit," then a mere boy, had his first experience with the Indians, and it was because of this fight the "Rock" received its name.

In those days the "Pawnees" were the most formidable tribe on the "Eastern Plains," and the freighters and trappers rarely escaped a skirmish with them either at the crossing of the "Walnut," "Pawnee Fork," or at "Little" or "Big" Coon creeks. To-day the historic hill looks down only upon peaceful homes and fruitful fields—where for hundreds of years it could tell of nothing but battle and death; where almost every yard of the brown sod at its base covered a grave; where there was nothing but shadow, now all is sunlight. In place of the horrid yell of the savage, as he wrenched the reeking scalp from his vanquished victim, the whistle of the locomotive and the pleasing whirr of the reaping machine is heard; where the death-cry of the painted warrior rang mournfully over the silent prairie, the waving grain is singing in beautiful rhythm as it bows to the summer breeze. Almost every day in the opening Spring, or before the grain-planting in the early fall, for several years during the first settlement of the country, in the vicinity of "Pawnee Rock," the skeletons of those killed there in the long years gone by—sometimes the bones of the white man, sometimes the bones of the red man—were plowed up; and even now, where new fields are opened, the "Rock" thus gradually unfolds the sphinx-like secrets of its dead. But of the fight from which "Pawnee Rock" took its name, and Carson's part in it:

It was late in the spring of 1833—"Kit" was then a mere boy, only seventeen years old, and as green as any boy of his age who has never been forty miles away from the place where he was born. Colonel Saint Vrain, a prominent agent of one of the great fur companies of that period, was fitting out an expedition at Ft. Osage, destined for the far off Rocky Mountains after the skins of the buffalo, beaver, otter, mink and other valuable fur-bearing animals that then roamed in immense numbers on the plains, or inhabited the hills at their western terminus, and to trade with the various tribes of Indians on the borders of Mexico.

This expedition young "Kit" joined, which was composed of twenty-six mule wagons, some loose stock and forty-two men. "Kit" was hired to help drive the extra animals, stand guard and make himself generally useful, which of course included fighting the Indians if any were met with on the route. The party left the fort one bright morning in May in excellent spirits, and in a few hours turned abruptly to the west on the broad trail to the mountains. The "Great Plains" in those years were solitary and desolate beyond the power of description; the Arkansas obeyed the tortuous windings of its treeless banks with a placidness that was awful in its very silence, and who followed the wanderings of that stream with no companion but his own thoughts realized in all its intensity the depth of that solitude which Crusoe suffered on his lonely island. Illimitable as the ocean, the weary waste stretched away until lost in the purple of the horizon, and the mirage created weird landcapes, and pictured distances that continually deceived and annoyed; but despite its loneliness, there was then, and ever has been, for most men, an infatuation and love for those majestic and inter-continental prairies that once experienced is never lost—and thus it came to the boyish heart of "Kit," so he never left them but with his life, and full of years.

There was not much change then, to the eternal sameness of things during the first two weeks, as the little expedition moved day after day through the wilderness of grass—its ever rattling wheels only intensifying the world of monotony surrounding. Occasionally, however, a herd of buffaloes were discovered in the dim distance, their brown shaggy sides contrasting strangly with the never ending sea of verdure around them; then "Kit" and two or three others of the party who were detailed to supply the teamsters and packers with fresh meat, would ride out after them on the best of the extra horses, which were always kept saddled and tied together behind the last wagon for services of this character. The buffalo quietly watched their coming until they were within a few hundred yards, and then giving three or four sniffs, with head raised, commenced their short, quick lope toward the bluffs; but "Kit" who was already an excellent horseman and a splendid shot with the rifle would soon overtake them, and topple one after another of their huge carcasses over on the prairie until a dozen or more were lying dead. The juicy humps, tongues and other choice portions were then cut off, put in a wagon which had by that time reached them from the train, and the expedition moved on.

So they marched on day after day for about three weeks when they arrived at the crossing of Walnut creek, where they saw the first sign of the Indian. They had halted for the day, the mules were unharnessed, the camp-fires lighted and the men about to indulge in their ever refreshing coffee, when suddenly half a dozen Pawnees, mounted on their ponies, hideously painted and uttering the most demoniacal yells rushed out of the tall grass on the river bottom—where they had been hiding—and swinging their blankets and robes attempted to stampede the herd, but the whole party were on their feet in a moment with rifle in hand; so all the Indians got for their pains were a few well deserved shots as they scampered back to the river and over into the sand-hills, and were soon out of sight.

The next night they camped at "Pawnee Rock," and of course after the experience of the evening before, every precaution was employed to prevent a surprise; the wagons were formed into a corral, so that the animals might be secured in the event of a prolonged fight; the guards were drilled, and every man slept with his rifle for a bed-fellow, for it was well known that the Indians would never rest satisfied with their defeat on the Walnut, but true to their thieving propensities and love of revenge would seize the first favorable opportunity to renew the attack.

"Kit" was posted immediately in front of the south face of the "Rock," nearly two hundred yards from the corral, and the others, who were on duty, at prominent points on top, and on the open prairie either side. About half past 11 o'clock some of the guard gave the alarm, "Indians!" and ran the mules into the corral, while the whole company turned at the report of a rifle on the midnight air, coming from the direction of the "Rock." In a few moments "Kit" came runing in to where the men had gathered and the colonel asked him if he had seen any Indians. "Yes," he replied, "I killed one of the red devils—I saw him fall." There was no further disturbance, it proved to be a false alarm; so the men were soon quietly sleeping, and "Kit" returned to his post. The next morning of course all were anxious to see "Kit's" dead Indian, and went out *en masse* to the "Rock," where, instead of finding a painted "Pawnee," they found "Kit's" mule—dead, shot through the head.

"Kit" felt terribly mortified over his ridiculous blunder, and it was a long time before he heard the last of his night raid on the mule; but he always liked to tell "the balance of the story," as he termed it, himself, and here is his version: "I did not sleep any the night before—I watched all the time to get a shot at the Pawnees that had tried to stampede our animals, and I suppose I felt a little sleepy leaning against those rocks—at any rate I was wide awake enough to hear the cry of 'Indian.' I had picketed my mule about twenty steps from where I stood, and I presume he had been lying down; all I know is that the first thing I saw after the alarm, was something rising up out of the grass, which I thought was an Indian—it was a center shot, I don't believe the mule ever kicked after he was hit."

The next morning the Pawnees attacked them in earnest, and kept the little command busy all that day, the next night, and until the midnight following—nearly three whole days—the mules all the time shut up in the corral without food or water. At midnight they hitched up and attempted to drive over the crossing of "Pawnee Fork" (where Larned is now situated). The trail at that point crossed the creek in the shape of a horse shoe—or, rather, in consequence of the double bend of the stream as it empties into the Arkansas, the road crossed it twice; in making this crooked passage many of the wagons were badly mashed up in the creek because the mules were thirsty and their drivers could not control them. The train was hardly strung out on the opposite bank when the Indians poured in a volley from both sides of the trail, but before they could reload and fire again, a charge was made among them headed by the Old Colonel, and it took only a few moments to "clean the Indians out" and the train moved on.

During the whole fight the little party lost four men killed, seven wounded, and eleven mules killed—not counting "Kit's"—and twenty wounded.

From this fight Pawnee Rock took its name, and it was there that "Kit Carson" had his first encounter with the Indians.

THE MARCH OF FRANCISCO VASQUEZ DE CORONADO,

IN SEARCH OF THE SEVEN CITIES OF CIBOLA AND THE KINGDOM OF QUIVIRA.

> "In the half forgotten era,
> With the avarice of old,
> Seeking cities that were told
> To be paved with solid gold,
> In the kingdom of Quivira—
>
> "Came the restless Coronado
> To the open Kansas plain;
> With his knights from sunny Spain,
> In an effort that, though vain,
> Thrilled with boldness and bravado."
> * * * * * * EUGENE WARE.

Many of our people are not aware, perhaps, that nearly three hundred and fifty years ago, or only forty-eight years after the discovery of America by Columbus, a large portion of Kansas was explored by the Spaniards. When we take into consideration the condition of the world at that period, and all the circumstances that surrounded the search of Coronado—which is the subject of this sketch—his journey into the then *terra incognita* of the central plains, stands as one of the grandest exploits recorded on the pages of history.

It appears that in the year 1530, during the time that

Nuño de Guzman was President of "New Spain," as all that territory acquired by the conquest of Cortez was then called, a slave of that high dignitary told his master some marvelous tales of a country far away in the north where were to be found cities and towns, so large and grand in their appointments that they rivaled even the splendor and wealth of Mexico, the capital of New Spain. This slave described in particular seven cities, whose streets were filled with shops, in which the workmen wrought in silver and gold exclusively; that these famous "seven cities" were located far beyond a great desert, through which it would require forty days to march. De Guzman, credulous as were all the Spaniards in those days, and ready to believe all the wonderful stories of the riches of the country they had come so far to conquer, immediately commenced the organization of a large force to discover the famous cities so minutely described by his slave. It is said that this expedition was composed of four hundred Spaniards and nearly twenty thousand Indians. *

The President commanded this rather formidable army in person, or at least until he reached Culiacan, for there his energy failed him, and he contented himself with simply establishing a colony. His excuse for relinquishing the search for the seven cities, was the "terrible and apparently interminable mountains over which he had to cross." Shortly after his abandonment of the expedition, his slave, who had

---

* There are many conflicting accounts of the number which composed this army and the above may be taken as within the limits of probability.

been the principal guide on the march as well, died, and with him perished for a while the story of the famous "Seven Cities," whose people were reveling in gold and silver.

Eight years afterward—in 1538—there came to the City of Mexico three Spaniards and an Arabian negro called Estivanico (Stephen). These three Spaniards, Alvar Nuñez Cabeça de Vaca, Andres Dorantes, Alonzo del Castillo Maldonado, and the negro, were the only survivors of the expedition of Pamphilo de Narvaez, about which I interpolate here a short extract from its history, as given by the early writers; not that it bears any direct relation to the "March of Coronado," but on account of the extraordinary adventures of these men.

They were part of a company who, with Pamphilo de Narvaez, sailed from the West Indies in the spring of 1528 to explore the country of Florida, of which the commander of the expedition, Pamphilo, had been made Governor. Pamphilo's command consisted of four hundred men and eighty horses. About the first of April he arrived in the harbor of Santa Cruz (now Tampa Bay), and early in May, with his little command, forty only of whom now were mounted, started for the interior of Florida. He marched constantly toward the North, keeping the coast in sight, and on the twenty-sixth of June reached the Indian village named Apuluche. Here he remained nearly a month, and then resumed his journey for more than a week, when he arrived at another village called Aute. He made a short halt at this place and then turned abruptly to the West. Marching in that direction for nearly a fortnight, his men became disheartened and dispirited in not finding any of the precious metals, and receiving nothing but insults and bad treatment from the Indians, the command retraced its steps to Aute, where, failing to glean any knowledge of the ships which had been ordered to follow them up the coast; they built five boats, in which all the party (who had not died or been killed by the Indians), now reduced to less than three hundred, sailed along the contour of the shore. In a few days they discovered the mouth of a swift running river, whose current was so strong they could make no headway against it, and their frail vessels were carried out into the Gulf.

About a week or ten days after their embarkation, while making slow journey toward the West, Cabeça de Vaca, in command of one of the boats, was wrecked on an island, which they immediately named Mulhado (misfortune). A few days after this mishap, all the remainder of the little fleet were capsized during a terrible storm off Mulhado, except that of Pamphilo, which drifted out to sea and was never heard from. All those who were not lost in this storm lived on the Island of Mulhado for more than six years, and were made slaves by the Indians, who treated them with the greatest cruelty. In consequence of the inhuman bearing of the savages toward them, and from starvation, most of the unfortunate Spaniards died.

After a weary and horrible six years of captivity, four of

them, (those men previously mentioned, and probably the only survivors of the whole party that were saved from the wrecks), escaped from the island and marched to the North, as far as the mountains of Alabama, from thence turned toward the setting sun and reached the Mississippi river—"the great river coming from the North"—as Cabeça called it. They continued on in a westerly direction, crossing the Arkansas and the Canadian at the great cañon of the latter river, from which point they turned to the southwest and passed through what is now New Mexico and Arizona to Culiacan, which province Guzman had already settled.

Upon reaching Culiacan, these remarkable men were full of strange stories and adventures, all of which were told to the Viceroy, then Don Antonio de Mendoca.

They stated to the Viceroy that the natives in some portions of the country through which they passed on their perilous journey, told them of rich and powerful cities, with houses four and five stories high, and that they were situated in the North.

Don Antonia de Mendoca communicated the strange stories and wonderful adventures of the newly arrived Spaniards to Francisco Vasquez de Coronado, the new governor, who immediately set out in person for Culiacan, and took with him three Franciscan friars, among whom was Marcos de Nica, a celebrated man in learning.

As soon as Coronado reached Culiacan, which journey he made with all possible haste, he ordered the three monks and the negro, Estévanico, to proceed on a voyage of discovery, and learn all they could in relation to the "seven cities," the story of which was now fully revived, eight years after the death of the Indian who had first mentioned their existence to the President de Guzman.

The three Spaniards left on their perilous mission in obedience to the order of the governor, but the negro, Stephen, becoming distasteful to them from some cause, they compelled him to go in advance to pacify the natives of the country through which he had passed on the memorable journey from the coast with Cabeça. It is related that as soon as Stephen reached the region of the "Seven Cities of Cibola" he made a demand of their people, not only for their wealth, but their women. In answer to this iniquitous demand the Indians killed him, and sent back some of the party that had come with him. These latter, the number not definitely known, frightened and demoralized at what they had seen, "went flying to their homes," but met the three friars in the desert some sixty leagues from Cibola. When the monks learned of the death of Stephen they became greatly frightened, and even distrusting the Indians who had gone out with Stephen, they made them presents of everything they had with them, excepting only the paraphernalia used in celebrating the mass, turned about, and by forced marches went back to Culiacan, knowing no more of the country than when they had set out, except what had been told them by the Indians.

When they reached Culiacan, they were immediately admitted to an audience with Coronado, to whom they gave a rose-colored tale of their own adventures; what Stephen had said, and also what the Indians had told them. They, also told Coronado of "islands filled with treasure, which, they were assured, existed in the 'Southern sea.'"

Coronado, after listening with enthusiastic delight to their marvelous tales, resolved to set out immediately for the city of Mexico to confer with the Viceroy, and took with him Friar Marcos de Niça, that the latter might tell in his own glowing language to the Viceroy in person all that had been told him.

Coronado must have been exceedingly credulous, and swallowed with avidity all the strange things he had heard, for he gathered a few of his most intimate friends, and to them alone disclosed what the old Friar had reported. He added to the story himself greatly, and exacted the strictest secrecy in relation to the wealth of the alleged famous "Seven Cities."

He arrived in Mexico in due season, and immediately closeted himself with the Viceroy, to whom he related the wonderful stories he had learned from Marcos de Nica and the others of his party. Coronado then proclaimed throughout that region that he had discovered the "Seven Cities of Cibola," and began to organize an expedition for their conquest.

Meanwhile Friar Marcos had been elevated through the influence of the church to the dignity of " Provincial of the

Franciscans" and their religious services were filled with the stories of the wonderful discoveries, which created such an enthusiasm, and coming from such a source, the infallible church, that volunteers offered their services in crowds, to the number, it is stated, of three hundred Spaniards and eight hundred Indians, all eager to march at once in quest of the famous "Seven Cities of Cibola." The majority of the Spaniards were of noble birth, and they met immediately and proclaimed Francisco Vasquez de Coronado, captain, in honor of the fact that he was the discoverer of the "Seven Cities," the objective point of the expedition.

The Viceroy Mendoca aided to the extent of the power, in preparing the little company for their hazardous enterprise, and appointed Compostella, a town some three hundred miles from Mexico, as the place of rendezvous, and the time, Shrove Tuesday. After this expedition had left the capital city, the Viceroy ordered Don Pedro d'Alarçon to leave for La Nativadad, a village on the coast, and in command of two small ships to proceed to Jalisco for the remainder of the supplies belonging to the expedition which the troops could not carry. The ships were then to follow the coast and keep pace with the army of Coronado, which it was thought from the received accounts of the direction it was to take, would always be along the sea. When all these preliminaries had been effected, the Viceroy departed for Compostella with a large retinue of noblemen, intending to review the army of Coronado in person, and give them such encouragement as his presence would naturally inspire.

This right royal cavalcade, with the Viceroy at its head, was received all along the route with the most distinguished consideration, and accorded that obsequious flattery which always bends to rank and station even in this age, in monarchical countries. When he arrived at Compostella he became the guest of Christoral de Onale, captain general of that province, and the next morning reviewed the troops comprising Coronado's little army, and after the celebration of the mass before the entire company made them a spirited address. After the Viceroy had pictured the wonderful results to be gained by this expedition, not only to themselves as individuals, in a pecuniary point of view, but to the renown and splendor of the Spanish throne, he requsted everyone to swear on a missal containing the Holy Evangelists, never to abandon their commander, no matter what might befall, and to implicitly obey all orders, and under all circumstances.

Early the next morning, with all the pomp and etiquette of royalty, Coronado gave the orders to move forward; seated on a magnificent stallion whose trappings were ornamented with gold and silver and emblazoned with symbols of the Spanish throne, he led his little army, which stepped proudly and confidently to the command of their general, toward the north. The Viceroy, accompanied by his retinue of generals and nobles, escorted the expedition as a mark of honor and encouragement, for two whole days, and then reluctantly retraced his steps to the capital. Almost immediately Coronado's army began to feel the effects of marching through a wild and unknown country; they were compelled to pack their baggage on the backs of their horses, and as this was a new experience it amounted to almost a complete failure. In wearily plodding over the ragged spurs and sharp ridges of the interminable ranges which they were obliged to cross, the animals would loose their foothold, and the packs, unskillfully tied on, lurching a little, would frequently throw its weight toward the side of the precipice, and down both horse and baggage would roll, for a thousand feet, perhaps, into the dark and rocky cañon below. It was no child's play, and each man of the little army, nobleman and common soldiers alike, took their turn in guiding the horses over the sinuous passage among the rocks and beetling cliffs. At last after a painful journey the expedition reached Chiametta, where it met Melchor Diaz and Juan de Saldibar, captains in the Spanish army, and a handful of determined soldiers, who had by a previous order of Coronado explored the country in advance of the main command as far as Chichilicese, on the edge of Friar Marco's "Desert" and some eight or nine hundred miles from Culiacan.*

Halting at Chiametta, to hear what report the Spanish captains, Diaz and Saldibar had to make in relation to their

---

* This distance is made up of estimates by myself, but all accounts of measurements in the narrative must be taken *cum grano salis*, as it is impossible in consequence of the incompleteness of the old maps to approximate correctness.

journeys, the soldiers and Indians of the command seized this opportunity of rest to fish, and to listen to the stories of their comrades around the camp-fires.

The next day after a secret interview between Coronado and the two captains, it was bruited among the rank and file that the account given of the country in the region of the "Desert," and the prospect from the top of the hills into that "Great Plain" was of the "most uncheerful and melancholy character," in consequence of which the troops became dispirited, and an atmosphere of discouragement settled upon the brave little band. We should not disparage this fact, however, for we must not entertain the idea for a moment, that anything like cowardice entered as a factor in the elements which made up the character of these men; we should rather remember that we are looking back through the dim vista of nearly four hundred years, and that not only the limited region which the love of conquest and spirit of adventure tempted them to enter, was an unknown country—but that the whole continent of America was an unexplored territory—a veritable *terra incognita* in fact—and it required a determination and energy, which even the boasted prowess of the nineteenth century might honorably shrink from. It was no wonder then, that this little band of Spaniards lost heart when the dismal and melancholy interview between the general and the captains—who had returned sick and desponding from their reconnoisance—spread through the camp.

But Friar de Niça disputed with Diaz and Saldibar; he

accused them of lying, and waxed wroth toward them in his harangues to the soldiers as they listened to him with that patience and attention due his exalted position in the Church. The Friar told them as they gathered around their camp-fires, that the country was fertile and abounded in precious metals; that they should not return without full reward for all their hardships, and that the world would yet ring with the story of their achievements.

The wily Friar thus under cover of his priestly garb restored them to a condition of obedience, and persuaded them by his elegant word-pictures—for history shows that he was an eloquent rascal—to continue their march in search of the "Seven Cities," which, he assured them had a veritable existence; this was on Easter Sunday, 1540, and on the next day the now freshly exhilarated little army took up its line of march for Culiacan. When they reached Culiacan the citizens turned out *en masse* to receive them, and showered upon Coronado a profusion of presents, to his followers they gave an abundance of fruits and supplies, and furnished them with everything necessary to continue their perilous journey into the "Desert."

Culiacan—where years before Nuna de Guzman established his colony—some seven hundred miles from Mexico—was the last place on the march inhabited by their own people, and the command remained here more than a fortnight to recuperate their worn-out horses, and make their last preparations for comfort, for from this point on there was no hope of succor, except what might possibly come from the natives, and these they knew nothing about, save from such tales as had been told them—the details of which, to say the least—were not by any means flattering, or held out much promise.

At the end of their somewhat protracted halt at Culiacan, Coronado made a new disposition of his forces, and deviated somewhat from his original programme. Taking fifty of his noblemen—his special personal friends—a portion of the foot-soldiers and all the monks, he left Culiacan after ordering the remainder of his army to wait until he had been gone a fortnight and then follow on his trail. Castenada, his historian, says: "When the General had passed through all the inhabited region to Chichilticale, where the desert begins, and saw that there was nothing good, he could not repress his sadness, notwithstanding the marvels that were promised further on. No one save the Indians who had accompanied the negro had seen them, and already they had been caught in lies. He was especially afflicted to find the Chichilticale, of which so much had been boasted, to be a single, ruined and roofless house, which at one time seemed to have been fortified. It was easy to see that this house, which was built of red earth, was the work of civilized people who had come from afar. On quitting this place they entered the desert. At the end of fifteen days they came within eight leagues of Cibola, on the banks of a river they called the Vermijo, on account of its red and troubled waters. Mullets, resembling those of Spain were found in it. It was there that the first Indians of the country were discovered; but when they saw the Spaniards they fled and gave the alarm. During the night of the succeeding day, when not more than two leagues from the village, some Indians who were concealed, suddenly uttered such piercing cries (the war-whoop?) that our soldiers became alarmed, notwithstanding, they pretended not to regard it as a surprise; and there were even some who saddled their horses the wrong way, but these were men who belonged to the new levies. The best warriors mounted their horses and scoured the country. The Indians who knew the land escaped easily and not one of them was taken. On the following day in good order we entered the inhabited country.

Cibola was the first village we discovered; on beholding it the army broke forth with maledictions on Friar Marcos de Niça. God grant that he may feel none of them. Cibola is built on a rock; this village is so small that in truth there are many farmers in New Spain that make a better appearance. It may contain two hundred warriors. The houses are built in three or four stories; they are small, not spacious, and have courts, as a single court serves for a whole quarter—the inhabitants of the province were united there. It is composed of seven towns, some which are larger and better fortified than Cibola. These Indians, ranged in good order, awaited us at some distance from the village. They were very loth to accept peace, and when they were required so to do by our interpreters, they menaced us by gestures; shouting our war-cry of Saint Iago, we charged upon them and quickly caused them to fly. Nevertheless it was necessary to get possession of Cibola, which was no easy achievement, for the road leading to it was both narrow and winding. The general was knocked down by the blow of a stone as he mounted in the assault, and he would have been slain, had it not been for Garci Lopez de Cardenas and Hernando d'Alvarado who threw themselves before him, and received the blows of the stones, which were designed for him and fell in large numbers; nevertheless as it is impossible to resist the first impetuous charge of Spaniards, the village was gained in less than an hour. It was found filled with provisions which were much needed, and in a short time the whole province was forced to accept peace." Coronado, as a good soldier should, immediately made his little command comfortable, and the strange and novel scenes among the natives sufficed to reconcile the troops for a while to the intense disappointment they had suffered, but a spirit of discontent and of desire for further exploration, inherent in the Spanish in those days, demanded constant work to keep them at all content.

Coronado, to control the element of discontent that again brooded over his command, organized little reconnoisances from his stronghold, into the neighboring districts, and hearing from one of his conquered Indians that there were seven other cities like those of Cibola, he ordered seventeen of his cavaliers and a few of the infantry under command of Don Pedro de Tobar, to search for them. A Franciscan monk, Friar Juan de Pudilla, who had once been a soldier himself, accompanied Don Pedro. In relation to this expedition of De Tobar's to this second group of "Seven Cities," the historian says: "The rumor had spread among their inhabitants that Cibola was captured by a very ferocious race of people, who bestrode horses that devoured men, and as they knew nothing of horses, this information filled them with the greatest astonishment. But notwithstanding all this, Don Pedro met with some show of resistance, and was obliged to make a series of charges among the infuriated savages, killing large numbers of them before he was permitted to take peaceable possession of the towns. When he had sufficiently overawed them by the powers of the Spanish armies—the terrible appearance of the horses, had as much to do with it as anything else—the savages hurried to their houses and begged him not to destroy them. They brought out presents of woven goods, fruits, corn, fowls, and a few precious stones as peace-offerings, which the Spaniards accepted, and began to question them of the country and its resources. They learned from these Indians, of a great river, on whose banks lived people who were immensely tall, and had dwellings much greater in all their proportions than the ones which they now looked on. With this information, Don Pedro returned to Cibola and imparted the information he had gathered to Coronado. Coronado immediately upon receipt of this intelligence, dispatched Don Garcie Lopez de Cardenas with a dozen men to explore the wonderful river spoken of by the Indians to Don Pedro.

De Cardenas apparently marched to the "seven cities" conquered where he was furnished with supplies by the natives, and from whom he evidently received further and correct information in relation to the "River."

Leaving the last mentioned towns, they wandered for nearly a month through a desert and reached a stream whose banks were so steep that, as the historian relates it, "they thought themselves elevated three or four leagues in the air." The adventurous little band marched for some days along the bank of the strange river, hoping to find some point at which they could descend to the water, which to them appeared only a few feet wide, but which in reality was a mile and a half, according to the declarations of the Indians.

At last after much weary and fruitless wandering, they reached a place where descent seemed practicable, and Melgosa Juan Galeras, and a private, who were the smallest men in the expedition, determined to make the attempt. They clambered down among the jagged points of rock until those above on the edge of the precipice could no longer see them.

Late in the afternoon the two venturesome men came back by the same path and reported their attempt a failure. They could not reach the water's edge, for what appeared above as small shelves of rock, were really huge masses with perpendicular walls sixty and a hundred feet high.

They only reached about one third of the distance, and from there the stream looked wide and confirmed the story of the Indians in relation to it. They assured their comrades that some of the rocks which from the top of the bank appeared no taller than a man, were in truth, higher and loftier than the tower of the Cathedral of Seville.*

Castenado says: "The river was the Tizon. A spot was reached much nearer its source, and that the Spaniards retraced their steps to Cibola, and this expedition had no other result. On their march back, they came to a waterfall with crystals of salt, large quantities of which they broke off and carried to Cibola.

During the absence of De Cardenas to the Great Cañon of the Tizon (Colorado River) some Indians whose homes were far to the east, arrived at Cibola. They called their country Cicuye, and were ruled over by a chief whose name was Bigotes, in consequence of his wearing huge mustaches. Bigotes came to Cibola with his subjects to offer his and their services to the Spaniards, of whom they had heard remarkable stories way off in their own province.

These Indians brought with them as presents to Coronado, skins, shields, and other articles, and in exchange for this courtesy, Coronado made them presents of necklaces of glass beads, and bells, and as the Indians had never seen such things before were much pleased as well as astonished.

One of the Indians told them of cows and showed the picture of one painted on his body.

---
*This was the Great Canon of the Colorado, where for hundreds of miles the cut edges of the table land rise abruptly, often perpendicularly, from the water's edge, forming walls from three to six thousand feet high.

Castenado says: "We would never have guessed it from seeing the skins of these animals, for they are covered with a frizzled hair which resembles wool."*

Coronado listened with marked attention to the story of Bigotes and his men, and called a council of his Cavaliers to listen and project another expedition to that region.

He appointed Captain Hernado d' Alvarado to the command with twenty men, and ordered them to go with the Indians, but to return in eighty days and make a report of what he might discover.

Alvarado made his preparations in a short time, and with his gallant little party, and Indians as guides, started on his enigmatical mission.

Castenado thus relates the march: "Five days after, they arrived at a village named Acuco, built on a rock. The inhabitants who are able to send about two hundred warriors into the field, are the most formidable brigands in the province. This village was very strongly posted, inasmuch as it was only reached by one path, and was built upon a rock precipitous on all its other sides, and at such a height that the ball from an arquebuse could scarcely reach its summit. It was entered by a strairway cut out by the hand of man, which

---

*This was the first idea the Spaniards received of the Buffalo, but they always speak of them as VACAS (Cows) as we shall see further on in our sketch when Coronado and his command reach the true Buffalo country—that is the Great Plains of Kansas.

began at the bottom of the declivitous rock, and led up to the village."

"The stairway was of suitable width for the first two hundred steps, but after these, were a hundred more much narrower, and when the top was finally to be reached, it was necessary to scramble up the three last *toises* by placing the feet in holes scraped in the rock, and as the ascender could scarcely make the point of his toe enter them, he was forced to cling to the precipice with his hands."

"On the summit there was a great arsenal of huge stones, which the defenders, without exposing themselves could roll down on their assailants, so that no army, no matter what its strength might be, could force this passage. There was on the top a sufficient space of ground to cultivate and store a large supply of corn, as well as cisterns to contain water and snow."

At this place the Indians were at first disposed to be hostile as they saw the Spaniards approach, and told them not to pass over a certain line they had marked on the ground, but as the latter paid no attention to the dictation and made preparations for battle, the Indians' bravado soon oozed out, and they brought presents of skins, nuts, flour and corn, and laid them at Alvarado's feet.

After resting at this village for a short time, and replenishing his little commissary with the best offerings of the Indians, Alvarado journeyed on, and in three days more reached another town called Tigeux whose people knowing Bigotes received the Spaniards very graciously.

Here Alvarado was so much gratified that he dispatched a courier back to Coronado, and suggested the propriety of the whole command coming to Tiguex and going into winter quarters.

Coronado was delighted when he heard the courier's report, and flattering himself that his difficulties were about ended, and the prospects brightening, he determined to act upon Alvarado's advice and move to Tiguex.

Alvarado, as soon as his messenger had departed to Cibola with the dispatch for Coronado, continued on his march for nearly a week, at the end of which time he came to another village called Cicuye. Cicuye was very strongly fortified and the houses four stories in height. Alvarado remained here some time to recuperate, and one day while idling through the town chanced to come upon "an Indian slave who was a native of the country adjacent to Florida."*

This slave, who was very communicative, the Spaniards nick-named Il Turco (the Turk) because he resembled so positively that class of people.

"Il Turco" was full of strange stories and adventures, to which the credulous Spanish, ready to believe anything, listened with the greatest earnestness.

He said there were great cities, and immense amounts of

---

* The name of Florida at that time was applied to all that tract of country from Canada to the river Del Norte.

gold and silver in his country, and beyond their extensive plains, over which roamed herds of cows so numerous that they could not be counted.

Alvarado, upon this, determined to make a journey to the buffalo country and take the slave with him as guide. He was absent some time, saw a few buffalo and then retraced his steps to Tiguex to report to Coronado, whom he supposed must have reached there by that time.

While Alvarado was making this series of little excursions from Tiguex, Coronado, who had started from Cibola, heard through some friendly Indians of eight other towns, so he determined to visit them on his march to Tiguex.

He selected thirty or forty of his most efficient soldiers, and leaving the main command to journey on, he made a detour in search of the reported eight cities. It appears that in ten or eleven days he found them in a province called Tutahaco but they did not compare even with the towns at Cibola, those having been built of stone, these of earth only. So diappointed, he set out for Tiguex.*

When Coronado reached Tiguex, he found Alvarado already returned from the buffalo country, and was much gratified by reports brought him by the Captain and "Il Turco," of that region.

Castenado says: "This Indian (the slave) told Coronado, that in his country there was a river two leagues wide, in which fish as large as horses were to be found; that there

---

* This portion of the journey is too ambiguous and I have severely let it alone.

were canoes with twenty oarsmen on each side, which were also propelled by sails; that the lords of the land were seated in the sterns upon a dais, while a large golden eagle was affixed to their prows. He added that the Sovereign of this region took his *siesta* beneath a huge tree to whose branches golden bells were hung which were rung by the agitation of the summer breeze."

He declared, morever, "that the commonest vessels were of sculptured silver; that the bowls, plates and dishes were of gold. He called gold *acochis*. He was believed because he spoke with great assurance, and because when some trinkets of copper were shown him, he smelt them and said they were not gold. He knew gold and silver well and made no account of the other metals."

"The General sent Hernando d'Alvarado to Cicuye to reclaim the golden bracelets which the 'Turk' pretended to have been taken from him when he was made prisoner. When Alvarado arrived there the inhabitants received him kindly, as they had done before, but they positively affirmed that they had no knowledge of the bracelets, and they assured him that the Turk was a great liar who deceived him."

"Alvarado seeing there was nothing else he could do, lured the Chief, Bigotes, and the Cacique under his tent, and caused them to be chained.

"The inhabitants reproached the Captain with being a man without faith or friendship, and launched a shower of arrows at him. Alvarado conducted these prisoners to

Tiguex, where the general retained them more than six months."

Let us turn to the main command of Coronado, which it will be remembered the General had left to make a detour.

It was sometime after Coronado had departed before the army, agreeably to orders, commenced its march for Tiguex. The command devolved upon Don Tristan d'Arellano, and on the first day out they came to the largest village yet seen. Here they camped, so well pleased were they with the surroundings.

Castenado says of this village: "There they found houses of seven stories, which was seen nowhere else. These belonged to private individuals, and served as fortresses. They rose so far above the others that they have the appearance of towers. There are embrasures and loop-holes, from which lances may be thrown, and the place defended. As all these villages have no streets, all the roofs are flat, and common for all the inhabitants; it is therefore necessary to take possession, first of all, of these large houses which serve as defenses."

When the army arrived at Tiguex it was received with demonstrations of welcome, and soon, like all soldiers, in the rest and good living, forgot all its troubles in getting there.

But soon the Spaniards through their own foolishness, commencing with that of Alvarado, just related, began to meet with disaster on every hand.

The action of Alvarado threw the whole province into

revolt, and the Spaniards after burning one or two small villages, and killing many of the inhabitants laid siege to Tiguex, which they did not succeed in capturing until after fifty days.

All the villages, one after another submitted, but the people left their homes and would not return to them while the now—and justly too—hated Spaniards remained in the country.

On the 5th of May, 1541, the earliest date at which the Tiguex river (the Rio Grande) was clear of ice, Coronado commenced his march for Quivira to look for gold and silver, which "Il Turco" had told them existed there in such large quantities. The army marched by Cicuye, and a few days after leaving the latter place they came to a river which was wide and swift and crossed a range of mountains near it. They called the river the Cicuye, and they were compelled to remain in camp on its banks while they built a bridge. In about two weeks after leaving this river, Coronado met the first genuine Indians of the plains. Their lodges were made of tanned cow (buffalo) skins, and they were called querechaos. It was here they saw their first buffalo, and the soldiers and cavaliers killed great numbers of them. It seems that after getting about nine hundred miles from Tiguex, the army finding itself with but little provisions left, Coronado ordered Don Tristan d'Arellano to fall back to Tiguex with the whole army, excepting thirty mounted, and six dismounted soldiers, whom Coronado took, and in command of this handful of men continued his search for Quivira.

The historian says: "The guides conducted the general to Quivira in forty-eight days, for they had traveled too much in the direction of Florida. At Quivira they found neither gold nor silver, and learning from the Turk that he had at the instance of the people of Cicuye purposely decoyed the army far into the plains to kill the horses, and thus make the men helpless, and fall an easy prey to the natives, and that all he said about the great quantity of silver and gold to be found was false, they strangled him."

"The Indians of this region, so far from having large quantities of gold and silver, did not know these metals. The Cacique wore on his breast a copper plate, of which he made a great parade, which he would not have done had he known anything about these precious metals."

The following quaint description is given of the Great Plains over which the exhausted Spaniards wandered after the treachery of Il Turco, and they were obliged to retrace their march to Tiguex half famished.* "From Cicuye they went to Quivira, which, after their account is almost three hundred leagues distant, through mighty plains, and sandy heaths so smooth and wearisome, and bare of wood that they made heaps of ox-dung, for want of stones and trees, that they might not lose themselves at their return: for three

---

* Hakluyt's Voyages, Vol. III. London 1600.

horses were lost on that plain, and one Spaniard which went from his company on hunting.

"All that way of plains are as full of crooked-back oxen, as the mountain Serrena in Spain is of sheep, but there is no such people as keep those cattle.

"They were a great succor for the hungry and want of bread which our people stood in need of.

"One day it rained in that plain a great shower of hail, as big as oranges, which caused many tears, weakness and bowes.

"Quivira is in forty degrees, it is a temperate country, and hath very good waters and much grass, plums, mulberries, nuts, melons and grapes, which ripen very well.

"There is no cotton, and the natives of that country apparel themselves with ox-hides and deer skins.

"Many of our people sought to have dwelt there, but Coronado would not consent, saying they could not maintain, nor defend themselves in so poor a country, and so far from succor.

"They traveled about nine hundred leagues in this country. All the way between Cicuye and Quivira is a vast plain without trees and stones, and hath but few and small towns.

"The men clothe themselves with leather, and the women, which are esteemed for their long locks, cover their heads with the same.

"They have no bread or any kind of grain, as they say, which I accounted a very great matter.

"Their chief food is flesh, and that oftentimes they eat raw, either of custom or for lack of wood. They eat the fat as they take it out of the ox, and drink the blood hot,* and do not die withal, though the ancient writers say that it killeth, as Empedocles and others affirmed. They drink it also cold dissolved in water.

"They seethe not the flesh for lack of pots, but roast it, or to say more properly, warm it at a fire of ox-dung; when they chaw their meat but little, and raven up much, and holding the flesh with their teeth, they cut with razors of stone which seemeth to be great bestiality; but such is their manner of living and fashion.

"They go together in companies, and move from one place to another, as the wild Moores of Barbary called Alarbes do, following the seasons and the pastures after their oxen.

"These oxen are of the bigness and color of our bulls, but their bones are not so great. They have a great bunch upon their fore-shoulder, and more hair on their fore part than on their hinder part, and it is like wool. They have as it were an horse-mane upon their backbone, and much hair and very long from their knees downward.

"They have great tufts of hair hanging down their foreheads, and it seemeth they have beards because of the great store of hair hanging down at their chins and throats.

---

* I have seen the Cheyennes eat the hot and quivering liver and fat torn from a freshly killed antelope when on a hunting party.—H. I.

"The males have very long tails, and a great knob or flock at the end, so that in some respects they resemble the lion, and in some other the camel.

"They push with their horns, they run, they overtake and kill an horse when they are in their rage and anger.

"Finally it is a foul and fierce beast of countenance and form of body.

"The horses fled from them, either because of their deformed shape, or else because they had never before seen them.

"Their masters have no other riches nor substance; of them they eat, they drink, they apparel, they shoe themselves, and of their hides they make many things, as houses, shoes, and apparel and ropes; of their bones they make bodkins, of their sinews and hair, thread; of their horns, mawes and bladders, vessels; of their dung, fire, and of their calves skins, budgets, wherein they draw and keep water. To be short, they make as many things of them as they have need of, or as many as suffice them in the use of this life.

"There are also in this country other beastes as big as horses, which because they have horns and fine wooll they are called sheep; and they say that every horne of them weigheth fifty pounds weight.*

"There are also great many dogs which will fight with a bull, and will carry fifty pounds weight in sacks when they

---

*This "beaste" is evidently the "Big Horn" of the Rocky Mountains, but the historian looked upon the animal with exaggerated optics.—H. I.

go hunting, or when they remove from place to place with their flocks and herds."

We will now follow the fortunes of the main army for a short time, which, it will be remembered, was sent back to Tiguex under Don Tristan d'Arellano, by the order of Coronado, on account of the scarcity of provisions.

The army was guided on its retreat to Tiguex by some natives who called themselves Teyans, and who promised to take them by a less circuitous route than the one they came. The historian thus relates the manner in which these Teyans guided the column: "Every morning they watched to note where the sun rose, and directed their way by shooting an arrow in advance, and then before reaching this arrow they discharged another; in this way they marked the whole of the route to the spot where water was to be found, and where they encamped.

"The army consumed only twenty-five days on their journey, and even then much time was lost. The first time it had taken thirty-seven days."

"On the road they passed a great number of salt marshes where there was a considerable quantity of salt. Pieces longer than tables and four or five inches thick were seen floating on the surface. On the plains they found an immense number of small animals resembling squirrels, and numerous holes burrowed by them in the earth."

Arellano arrived at Tiguex in July, 1541, and sent out

another expedition under Captain Francisco de Barrio-Nuevo to ascend the river (Rio Grande).

On their march they found a large village which the inhabitants called Braba, but which the Spaniards re-christened Valladolid. "It was built on the two banks of the river which was crossed by bridges built with nicely squared timber."

Still another expedition was sent by Arellano south from Tiguex, for about three hundred miles, where they found four more villages, and "reached a place where the river plunged beneath the ground; but, inasmuch as their orders confined them to a distance of eighty leagues, they did not push on to the place where, according to the Indians' accounts, this stream escapes again from the earth with considerable augmented volume."

Meanwhile, Don Tristan d'Arellano became alarmed for the safety of Coronado who should have returned by this time according to his express declarations, so the Don set out in search of him in person, taking with him forty of his cavaliers. When he reached Cicuye, the Indians rushed out and attacked him, in which skirmish he lost some men, and was delayed a week. Just as he was ready to move forward again, some of the natives, who had just returned from a hunting expedition, told him that Coronado was coming, and he remained in camp, holding the Indians at bay until the general arrived, after which they all went back to Tiguex.

When Coronado reached Tiguex, he put the whole command—which was now together once more—into winter quarters.

"When winter was over Coronado ordered the preparation to be made for the march to Quivira. Every one then began to make his arrangements, nevertheless, as it often happens in the Indies, things did not turn out as people intended, but as God pleased. One day of festival the general went forth on horse-back, as was his custom, to run at the ring with Don Pedro Maldonado. He was mounted on an excellent horse, but his valets having changed the girth of his saddle, and having taken a rotten one, it broke in mid-course, and the rider unfortunately fell near Don Pedro, whose horse was in full career, and in springing over his body, kicked him in the head, thus inflicting an injury which kept him a long time in bed and placed him within two fingers of death.

"The result of this was that, being of a superstitious nature, and having been foretold by a certain mathematician of Salamanca, who was his friend, that he should one day find himself the omnipotent lord of a distant country, but that he should have a fall that would cause his death, he was very anxious to hasten home and die near his wife and children."

This so worked upon Coronada, says the historian, that he feigned to be more ill than he really was, and he thus worked upon the army as to induce them to petition him to return to New Spain. They began openly to declare that, inasmuch as there had been no rich country discovered, it was better to abandon any further search.

Coronado, upon the development of this spirit among his soldiers, which he himself had mainly brought about, turned his line of march to Mexico, passing through Cibola and other places on his journey out.

Coronado met with some resistance, and had many of his men and horses killed on the route.

On his arrival in the City of Mexico, he was received with ill-grace by the Viceroy, says the historian, but, nevertheless, he received his discharge, yet he lost his reputation, and soon after his government of New Galicia also.

Thus ended the great expedition which was fruitless in its search for Quivira or for gold.

Now, let us determine, if possible, the route of Coronado, and what points on the Great Plains we can, with some degree of reason, declare he visited.

Civola, or Cibola is the name by which the Mexicans designate the buffalo or bison.

It is defined in Newman's Dictionary Cibola or Civola, a quadruped called the Mexican bull. It seems to have had that name in Mexico before the conquest of Cortez, and that a skeleton of one was among Montezuma's collection of curiosities. But there were none within eight hundred miles of the boundary of the Mexican civilization.

At all events Cibola or Civola meant the buffalo country, and it is quite possible that the place now known as Quivira, was the true Quivira of the Indians at the time of Coronado's march. But whether deceived by the treacherous Indian guide—whom they strangled, as related—or having misunderstood what the Indian meant, the Spaniards gave the name of Quivira to an imaginary country situated far north and reported abounding in gold, and which Coronado visited.

Starting with the march from Tiguex, the first important place was Cicuye.

The historian says: "After a journey of five days from Tiguex, Alvarado arrived at Cicuye a very well fortified village, the houses of which are four stories high". * * * Cicuye is built in a narrow valley in the midst of mountains covered with pines. It is traversed by a small stream, in which we caught some excellent trout."

Mr. E. S. Squier, Mr. Kern, and Col. Simpson have determined the ruins of Pecos on the Rio Pecos to be the Cicuye of Coronado.* They are "situated in a narrow valley in the midst of pines, and the site is traversed by a small silvery stream in which can be found some excellent trout," says the historian.

I well remember now nearly fifteen years ago, I gazed with strange feelings the first time upon the ruins of Pecos. It was early morning in October, and the wind blew delicious

---

*The ruins on the Rio Pecos have been visited by the writer a dozen times or more, and each time the proof accumulates that here was located the Cicuye of Coronado, and not at Santa Fe, as some here declare. The records of the Catholic church, and the priests themselves indorse it, but still it will remain an open question I suppose.—H. I.

and crisp from the tops of the silvery pines piled up in the rocky cañons on either side. I remember how my thoughts wandered back in the shadowy past, when the dead and forgotten civilization now in ashes under my feet was busy with the music of life. I fancied I could almost see the little band of determined Spaniards on their strange march over the rugged hills, and as I pulled off pieces of the blue fresco from the walls of the old church it seemed as fresh as if painted yesterday instead of nearly four hundred years ago, while the town itself ante-dates the church at least a thousand years.

The rudely carved beams here and there sticking out from detached portions of the ruin were as sound as if cut that morning from among the towering pines all around me. I thought too of Coronado and his "excellent trout" as I sat down to breakfast on half a dozen—just pulled from the water—in the old adobe ranch of Kosloskie, the generous Pole, who has lived on that classic spot for a quarter of a century. If any who have ever traveled from Fort Union to Santa Fe within the last twenty years should see these lines, they will recall the wild scenery, and particularly the magnificent trout, always to be found at every meal in the old ranch on the Pecos.

I have not deemed it advisable to enter into a discussion of the exact locality of all the places visited by Coronado and his adventurous little army, because of the space it would require to do the subject justice, and because of the more important fact that they lie beyond the geographical area of our state, and are not germane really to the design of this sketch—the march of Coronado into Kansas. Therefore, however interesting it may be, and really is, to the student of history, the story of the march will be limited to Kansas, and the territory immediately contiguous.

Quivira, "the last place visited by Coronado," says the historian. Where was Quivira? has been a fruitful source of discussion among geographers for the past half century.

"Coronado appears to have proceeded as far north as near the fortieth degree of latitude, in search of Quivira," says Mr. Gallatin.

Colonel Simpson, an excellent authority, says: "Now it is something singular, so far as I have been able to investigate, there is no such place as Quivira laid down on the old maps in the locality where modern maps show it—namely in latitude thirty-four, longitude one hundred and six; but there is a place of that name laid down on the maps in about latitude forty, as far as Coronado located it. I am, therefore, inclined to believe that at the time of Coronado's expedition the former Quivira did not exist. At all events, it is scarcely credible that such a remarkable city as Quivira was represented to be, so full of gold, etc., situated as it was, *only about fifty miles from Tiguex*, the headquarters of Coronado's army, and which might have been reached in two days, could have been kept from the knowledge and observation of the army for about a year and a half, during all the time that a portion of it was stationed at that place."

Gregg in commenting on the antiquity of the Quivira as laid down in the modern maps—latitude thirty-four—says: "By some persons these ruins have been supposed to be the remains of an ancient Pueblo or the Aboriginal City. That is not probable however, for the relics of aboriginal temples might possibly be mistaken for these Catholic churches, yet is it not perceived that the Spanish Coat of Arms would be found sculptured and painted on their façades, as is the case in more than one instance ?"

Coronado says: "The province of Quivira is nine hundred and fifty leagues * * from Mexico. The place I have reached is the fortieth degree of latitude. The earth is the best possible for all kinds of productions of Spain, for while it is very strong and black, it is well watered by brooks, springs and rivers. I found prunes like those of Spain, some of which were black, also some excellent grapes and mulberries. Following the orders of your majesty I have observed the best possible treatment toward the natives of this province, and of all others that I have traversed.

"They have nothing to complain of me or my people. I sojourned twenty-five days. in the province of Quivira, as much as to thorougly explore the country as to see if I could not find some further occasion to serve your majesty, for the guides whom I have brought with me have spoken of provinces still further on. That which I have been able to learn is, that in all this country one can find neither gold nor any other metal. They spoke to me of small villages, whose inhabitants for the most part did not cultivate the soil. They have huts of hides and of willows, and change their places of abode with the *vaches* (buffaloes). The tale they told me then (that Quivira was a city abounding in gold) was false. In inducing me to part with all my army to come to this country, the Indians thought that the country being desert and without water, they would conduct us where our horses and ourselves would die of hunger; that is what the guides have confessed. They told me that they had acted by the advice of the natives of these countries."

Jaramillo who was one of the few selected by Coronado to accompany him on his long march to Quivira says:

"This country has a superb appearance, and such that I have not seen better in all Spain, neither in Italy, nor France, nor in any other country where I have been in the service of your majesty. It is not a country of mountains; there are only some hills, some plains, and some streams of very fine water. It satisfies me completely. I presume that it is very fertile and favorable for the cultivation of all kinds of fruits."

Castenado says: "It is in this country that the Espiritu Sancto,* which Don Ferdinand de Soto discovered in Florida, takes its source."

"The course of this river is so long, and it receives so many affluents, that it is of prodigious length to where it de-

---
* The Mississippi.

bouches into the sea, and its fresh waters extend far out after you have lost sight of the land."

Coronado writes of another large river with a smaller one flowing into it. He called these the Saint Peter and Saint Paul.

I am inclined to believe that these two rivers were the Arkansas, and the Little Arkansas.

He also speaks of viewing a large river called the "Teucarea."

This was the Missouri, and he gazed upon it in all probability from the spot on which Atchison now stands—but of this further on.

Taking into consideration the fact that New Mexico is mountainous, and that Coronado could only have met with such a region as he discovers—its richness and blackness of soil, the various fruits which he says grew spontaneously—on the Great Plains, there can no longer be any doubt of the route of his march.

How familiar it sounds—"Mighty plains and sandy heaths so smooth and wearisome"—a perfect description of the mighty stretch of country from the foot of the mountains eastward.

His route was beyond doubt in a northeasterly direction from Cicuye (Pecos), and after reaching the vicinity of the thirty-seventh parallel, turned nearly due east, and marched constantly south of the Arkansas until he arrived at the junction of the Arkansas and the Little Arkansas—where Wichita now stands. Taking into consideration the probable error of his instruments, he certainly crossed between Hutchinson and Wichita.

He speaks of the two rivers which he called Saint Paul and Saint Peter, and could not have known of the existence of the Little Arkansas if he had crossed below it.

Take a map and fold it, so that a line is drawn from the thirty-seventh parallel of latitude (where it intersects the one hundred and third meridian of longitude*) and the plicature will pass directly through the extensive salt plains of the Cimarron, and cut the Arkansas at Wichita; this was undoubtedly the line of Coronado's march, and the mouth of the Little Arkansas was the point of separation from the main army, for it will be remembered that about thirty-seven days eastward from Tiguex, the provisions failing, the major portion of the command were obliged to retreat toward the latter place, while Coronado with a select number—only thirty-six or forty in all—of his cavaliers, continued their journey toward the north—still in search of the mythical Quivira—the "land abounding in gold and other precious metals."

Let us fancy the shadow on the sun-dial of the ages moved backward for nearly four hundred years, and ourselves standing on the bank of the beautiful "Little River" where it gurgles and splashes over the rounded pebbles, as it pours out its contribution of sweet water to that "silent stream" whose sand-reaches, and dark eddies constantly pick up more

---
*From Greenwich.

and more of the infiltrated rain drops on its restless way to the sea.

Under the leafiest of the grand old cottonwoods which fringed its grassy border—for there were gnarled and tempest riven old cottonwoods in those days of the shadowy past—reclined on the velvety sod, with a score or more of Spain's proudest nobles around him, Coronado—the man of visions; the pursuer of a phantom; the dreamer—building his hopes out of such stuff as nightmares are created.

His thoughts, perhaps, wandered back to the splendor of that court which gave new worlds to men like him, and as the soft spring breeze from the south toyed with his dark curls, ambition was still at work beneath, leading him on, till it should overleap itself and crush him with the remorselessness of a demon.

Listlessly, with the mutterings of mutiny only half choked down, in little groups all around him on the fresh sod, sat the rank and file of his adventurous band.

The blue and white anemones in the beauty of their unfolding, reflected the gorgeous tint above them, but had no charms for the half-starved and awe-stricken soldiers who had been deceived by the treacherous guides, and lured into the wilderness that there perhaps they might find their death.

With fear and trembling they gazed upon the magnificent picture before them, but its gorgeous colors were black to them, and like "Dead Sea fruit," all they touched was only ashes to their mental lips.

Coronado held a council with his nobles, and it was deemed wise that most of them should go back, as bootless of results as when they started.

With heavy heart he listened to the counsels of his cavaliers, and reluctantly issued the order which, in a measure at least, dashed the cup of his ambition to the ground and shattered it into a thousand fragments.

The next morning after the deliberations under the cottonwood, his army was drawn up in line, and he made them a strong appeal to remain faithful to the awful oath they had taken at Compostella, and bade them farewell; then, as all but his few picked friends, who had chosen to follow the fortunes of their commander still further into the wilderness, slowly wound their way through the fringe of timber westward, he mounted his black charger, and with an imperious wave of his hand to the north, started in that direction, still seeking the Alnaschar of his dreams.

Returning to the outward march of the command from Tiguex, and before they reached the point of separation—as I believe the mouth of the Little Arkansas, as stated—it will be remembered the historian says: "On the road they passed a great number of salt marshes, where there was a considerable quantity of salt."

These salt ponds or marshes are only to be found in the region of country between the Arkansas and the Canadian, through which the plicatures in our folded map pass. I do not mean that the route is directly east from the intersection of the thirty-seventh parallel with the one hundred and third meridian, but that the trail of Coronado has an eastern trend from that point, and passing through the salt marshes of the Cimarron, terminates at Wichita, or he could not have seen the two rivers as the historian relates he did, at any other point. If he passed below—to the east of Wichita—he would have missed the Little Arkansas completely, and if he crossed the Arkansas proper, west of the junction of the two rivers, he could only have crossed the Little Arkansas where it is an inconsiderable stream, not worthy the dignity of the name of St. Paul.

Coronado crossed the Kaw, I am inclined to believe, a short distance east of the ninety-seventh meridian of longitude, or near where Abilene is now located.

From thence he went to the high bluffs overlooking the city of Atchison, and gazed upon the "great river" "Teucarea"—the Missouri.

The most exalted spot overlooking the river at this point is where the residence of our distinguished Senator, Hon. J. J. Ingalls stands, and it is not improbable the beautiful vista which presents itself from the windows of that modest, but cultivated home, greeted Coronado's eyes, nearly four hundred years ago.

There upon the rugged cliffs above Atchison, the dream of Coronado came to an end, and bitter must have been the disappointment, and terrible the wreck of his ambition, as he gazed upon the muddy flood at his feet.

The province of Quivira—the mythical Quivira, so far as it was a land "abounding in gold and other precious metals," extended from the thirty-ninth to the forty-first degree of latitude north and south, and from the ninety-fifth to the ninety-seventh degree of longitude, east and west. This was about its geographical area, according to the old maps, but Coronado did not go beyond where Atchison now stands, or about half way between its northern and southern limit.

There, as he gazed upon the turbulent Missouri—the Teucarea of the Indians—he saw that it was useless to proceed further toward the north.

The interminable woods stretching out before him had their legends of horror, and his naturally superstitious mind, already surfeited with terrible experiences, and confidence in his guides completely lost, there was nothing left for him to do but to return to Mexico—baffled, defeated and crushed with disappointments.

It is difficult to trace with accuracy the whole of the return march of Coronado, in consequence of the obscurity of the narrative and appellations of localities, which if they ever had a veritable existence, have been lost in tradition during the long interval of time since the date of that memorable expedition.

Whether he returned to the "point of separation"—the mouth of the Little Arkansas—or followed the tortuous line of the Kaw, and thence westward through the bluffs of the Smoky-Hill to some locality where he suddenly turned to the south, (which theory I adopt) must apparently remain a mystery, unless in time to come, some now lost, and musty old record, shall be discovered that will offer a solution to the problem.

We can, therefore, only speculate, and base our conclusions upon the meager facts attainable, and depend almost entirely upon presumptive evidence to make out a route, which at best, is only mere guess work, until we find him again south of the Arkansas, and near the mountains.

My reason for thus defining the probable return march of Coronado, are based upon the fact, that on Big Creek in Ellis county, there is a huge mass of detached rock, on which as late as 1869, could be discovered a series of rude carvings, among which was the Spanish Coat of Arms, the Spanish flag and a date, which though almost illegible, the figures fifteen—for the century—could be still traced, but the year had become obliterated. The names cut under the flag were illegible beyond hope of deciphering, as was all the other chiseling evidently connected with the whole legend.

I am inclined to believe that Coronado reached his maximum northern point at about where Atchison now stands, and that from thence he followed the Missouri south, until he reached the mouth of the Kaw, where he turned abruptly and marched along its northern bank, until he came to the Solomon or North Fork of the Smoky-Hill.

He then crossed that stream and the Saline, continuing along the north bank of the Smoky Hill until Big Creek was reached, from whence he turned abruptly south and crossed the Arkansas between Kinsley and where the new town of Cimarron, in Ford county, is now located.

I am not aware whether the rock on Big Creek is in existence to-day or not, or if it is, whether the rude carving referred to is longer legible. Neither can it be determined with any degree of certainty, whether the names and date which could be seen as late as I have stated, were those of Coronado's little band. We have to accept it as mere presumptive evidence, coupled with the idea that Coronado would hardly choose to return by the same route he had followed on his outward march.

If he actually marched over the route I have described, and believe probable, I deduce the idea, that on his arrival at Big Creek he turned abruptly toward the south or rather southwest, from the fact that where Ellsworth in Ellsworth county is located, the Smoky Hill reaches its most southern latitude —from that point it gradually trends to the northwest, and that Coronado observing this (by the use of his instruments) made a tangent with it of his line of march, because he saw it (the trend of the river) was leading him away from the true course he desired to take.

It was perfectly natural too, that at the point of leaving his course he should leave some evidence of the fact, and more probable that this evidence should be his name, the names of the most prominent of his followers, and the flag under which he served, cut on the enduring rock.

That this was the habit of Coronado and all the early Spanish explorers, we have only to refer to their routes through Mexico, Arizona and New Mexico, where whenever a surface of wall presented itself, there, we find a record of the march and its date cut in hard rock.

Coronado evidently moved in a south-westerly direction from his place of departure on the Smoky Hill, for we know that he crossed his outward trail south of the Arkansas, and his objective point (Tiguex) lying in the prolongation of that line, he could have taken no other course.

His route passed near the Antelope hills (in Texas) a little west of which he crossed the Canadian, and thence south-westerly to the Pecos, which he crossed, and marched north-westerly to Cicuye (now the ruins of Pecos) heretofore described where we will leave him.

Thus it appears Coronado traversed the State of Kansas, diagonally, twice—in going out, and returning from Quivira, and that he followed for a long distance, the course of what in after years was known as the "Santa Fe trail," and was therefore the first white man who traveled that great and historic highway.

He and his little band of cavaliers have made many localities classic ground, yet strange as it may seem, none have seen fit to do his memory honor.

An attempt was made some years since by Geo. W. Martin, I believe, to change the name of Davis county to that of Coronado.

The explorations of Coronado extended over two years, and must be regarded as one of the grandest expeditions of modern times.

Although fruitless in results so far as beneficial discoveries were concerned, it convinces us of the indomitable and unconquerable spirit of conquest by which the Spaniards were imbued, and places them at that period of the world at the head of all nations in intelligence and power.

It would be interesting to follow the fortunes of that other expedition up the sea-coast, which was part in reality of Coronado's, but, we have refrained for all but a mere allusion to it, because it is not within the province of what was intended in this sketch.

In conclusion, I shall give the historian's idea of the origin of the people whom they met on their route through New Mexico, to show how crude the opinion extant at that time was of the geography of the continent:

"These nations, which are so entirely different from those of all the other nations we have found up to the present time, must have come from the region west of the Great India, where its coasts, touch those of this country on the west.

"According to the route they followed they must have come from the extremity of the Eastern India, and from a very unknown region, which, according to the information of the coast, would be situated far in the interior of the land betwixt China and Norway. There must, in fact, be an immense distance from one sea to the other, according to the form of the coast as it has been discovered by Captain Villalobos, who took that direction in seeking for China. The same occurs when we follow the coast of Florida; it always approaches Norway up to the point where the country 'des baccalaos,' or codfish is obtained."

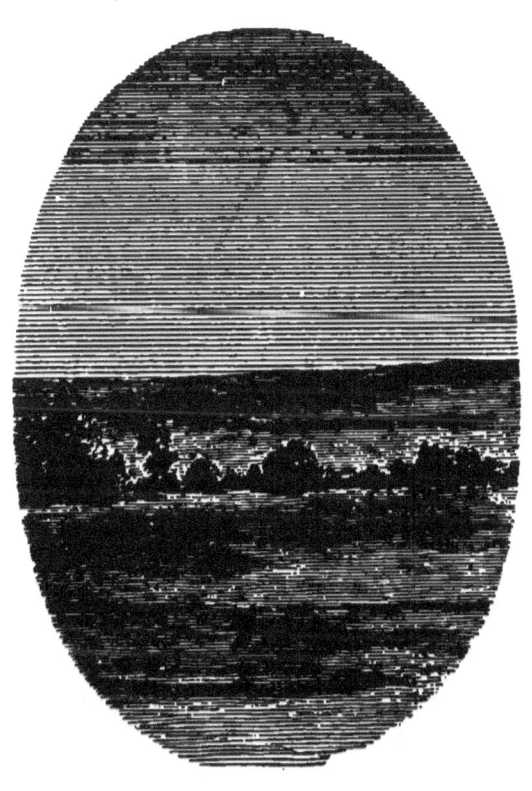

THE LEGEND OF TEPEYACAC.

The 12th of December is remarkable in the religious calendar of New Mexico as the anniversary of a miraculous visit of the Virgin to an uneducated and simple Indian, who comes down to us on the pages of history as Juan Diego—a hero in every sense of the word, according to the estimate placed upon him by the thousands and tens of thousands who in the long centuries that have passed have worshiped at the shrine, his story and the wonderful confirmatory proof that accompanied it, he left them as a precious legacy.

That Juan Diego was the recipient of a veritable visit from the Virgin, is as earnestly and honestly believed in by the Catholic world of both Old and New Mexico as the most simple and plausible tenet of their church, and it would be as presumptuous to discredit it as to doubt the existence of the Virgin herself.

The legend boasts of considerable antiquity; dating back to a certain Saturday, December 9th, 1531, only a short period after the City of Mexico had been selected as the residence of that first Bishop (Senior Don Francisco de'Zumarraga) who emulating Alexander, destroyed in the same manner, the invaluable archives of the country he presided over with the title of "Protector of the Indians" in addition to that of his apostolic one. Juan Diego was well deserving the honors conferred upon him by one of the holy family, if we are to accept the ingredients of character accorded to him; for he is represented as "recently converted, of pure and unblemished morals, though of lowly birth."

It was early morning, and the scarped side of Tepeyacac * reflected the golden sunlight as it streamed in rich floods across the dark valley still hushed in the gloomy shadow of Popocatapetl, but around whose icy summit played a most gorgeous iridescence as the rays glinted from crag to pinnacle. Juan Diego deeply impressed with the importance of his religious obligations, had long since risen from his humble bed, and was well on his way to attend the celebration of the mass which the monks of his district directed daily at that early hour, and had just reached the summit of the little path that ran over Tepeyacac when his meditations were interrupted by "a sweet, sonorous and harmonious music, as of little birds." The soft strains and rare melody he could not resist, and looking about him to divine the cause of the heavenly concert, "he saw a white and shining cloud surrounded by a rainbow, and in its center a most beautiful lady." Almost prostrated at the enchanting vision before him he

---

* "Tepeyacac is a small mountain whose southern side is an inaccessable precipice, which looks to the City of Mexico, situated on the south of it at the distance of about three miles. Its ascent by whatever part undertaken, except that of the pathways made to facilitate the access, is extremely rough and stony. Its whole surface is covered with crowfeet, buck and hawthorn, which are common to such sterile wastes. The Aztec name, Tepeyacac, signifies the abrupt extremity or termination of hills; and in this bluff terminate all the hills to the north of the Capital. *Mayer, Vol. I.*

dared not gaze upon it until he was assured by a soft and beautiful voice, addressing him in his own language "not to be afraid," that she who was conversing with him was "the Virgin Mary, the mother of God," whose mass he was on his way to hear. "She commanded him to go to the Bishop and tell him that it was her will that a temple should be built to her upon that spot, in which she would show herself a pious mother toward him, his nation, devotees, and as many as should solicit her support and protection in their hour of need." Juan listened earnestly in an attitude of profound devotion, and crossing himself was about to leave the sacred spot when the lovely apparition motioned him to stop and hear all she had to say; continuing the lady said: "Be sure, my son, for whom I feel a delicate and tender love, that I will repay all you do for me; I will render you famous; and will endow you with benefits for the diligence and labor you display. Now, my servant, in whom I delight, thou hast heard my desire, go thou in peace."

Juan intoxicated with the rapturous vision he had witnessed, forgetting, or rather delayed beyond the hour to say his matins at the little church, for which he started out on his early journey, immediately wended his way over the mountain and down into the valley where he struck the broad highway leading into the city, nor did he stop again until he reached the palace gate, within which resided the venerable and illustrious archbishop, and with whom he immediately craved an interview.

After a few moments parleying with the servants, who were loth to disturb their master at that early hour, the prelate who was in his study, hearing the commotion outside, himself came forth, and being importuned by Juan, who was invited by the archbishop to enter the palace, when Juan, all excitement, poured forth his strange story. The worthy man was both incredulous and startled, as Juan related all the marvelous things he had seen, and repeated with emphasis the mission the wonderful apparition had delegated to him. The bishop attempted to reason with him upon the possibility of what he alleged to have seen, which might only have been a creation of his brain, induced by the holy thoughts that filled his mind, while on his way to his morning devotion, but upon Juan's insisting that what had appeared was as tangible as the presence of the holy father before him, the latter urged him to return to his home, and he would consider what it was best for one to do who had been so favored above all men, and that at some future day, after meditation and prayer upon the subject, he would farther advise him.

Juan submissive, but not altogether inclined to act strictly according to the injunctions of the bishop, and with the impressions of his remarkable adventure of a few hours before not by any means effaced from his memory, instead of repairing to his own home, as he had been enjoined, found himself irresistibly drawn toward the little mountain, and to the spot where his eyes had feasted upon the lovely picture. He was not surprised to find the Most Holy Virgin in the same place where he had first seen her, and apparently waiting his coming. Kneeling reverently before her, and in most submissive language, he told her of his visit to the bishop, and all that had transpired at the interview with that righteous man, and urging that it were better if she would delegate her wishes to some not so lowly and humble as he, feared he would not be credited with truthfulness, "because he was an humble man and a plebeian." The Virgin regarding him with the greatest benignity, and smiling upon him in the most heavenly manner, replied: "To me neither servants nor followers whom to send are wanting if I should wish, since I have multitudes at my command; but it is agreeable to me now that *thou* shouldst perform this mission and make the solicitation. Through your intervention I wish to give effect to my will, and desire you to speak again with the bishop, and tell him he must build a temple in honor of me on this spot; and that it is the Most Holy Virgin Mary, Mother of the true God, who sends you."

Juan filled with the best and purest thoughts his deeply religious nature was capable of, and wonderfully impressed with the favor that had been accorded him, though realizing the awful majesty of the Holy presence before him, tremblingly answered: "Do not be offended, my Queen and Holy Lady, at what I have said, which is not intended to excuse me from this office, I hereby pledge myself to repeat what you have instructed me to say, to the bishop, and I promise, that at the setting of the sun to morrow I will be here with his reply."

Juan then in an attitude of the profoundest humility took leave again of the entrancing vision, and returned to his own home, sad and sorrowful, for he felt that the bishop would not give credence to his story, and he would suffer the displeasure of the Holy Mother on the morrow.

The next day was Sunday, December 10th, 1531, and our devoted Indian attended mass at an early hour as usual, at the conclusion of which, realizing what terrible judgment might be visited upon him, should he neglect in the slightest particular his promised pledge of the day before, he immediately set himself about the fulfillment of that obligation.

Hastening then, he soon reached the gate of the bishop's palace, where as before, he begged he might be admitted to his presence. But as on the previous occasion, the servants hesitated to give the poor man entrance, and it was only after a series of earnest importunity they allowed him to go in.

Throwing himself upon the floor before the bishop, and earnestly imploring that dignitary to listen to him, he with the deepest emotion related his second experience on the mountain. His rude eloquence and impressive manner touched the heart of the holy prelate, and lifting Juan up tenderly he embraced him ; and with tears in his eyes catechised him carefully, but found no prevarication or deviation from a straightforward and apparently true tale. He encouraged Juan, and told him, that although he believed that he, Juan, had really seen some remarkable vision, still it was not sufficiently well established for him to take immediate action upon, he therefore advised that he should go back to where he had seen the apparition, and if the lady made her appearance again, he should ask for a *sign*, through which it might be known to the Church, that the "Mother of God" had really sent him.

Juan, with the innate consciousness of the truth of his statement to the bishop, thanked him, and told him he would do all that he desired of him, and with a comparatively light heart he left the palace. The Bishop observing that Juan had departed from his presence in an entirely different state of mind from that in which he had entered, and believing that he would follow out his instructions explicitly in relation to asking of the party with whom he alleged having conversed on the mountain, for some sign, quietly ordered two of his confidential servants secretly to watch Juan's movements, and find out without being discovered, who it was he would speak to on his arrival at the top of Tepeyacac. These spies kept close on the trail of the Indian until he reached the foot of the sacred hill, when he suddenly disappeared, and all their efforts to find him were unavailing, although they diligently searched every ravine and portion of the mountain in which it was possible for a man to secrete himself. Disgusted, and weary with much walking, they returned to the palace and reported to the bishop that Juan was an imposter, and that no credence should be given to his fabulous stories.

Juan, however, oblivious to the fact that he had been watched and to the unwelcome report that had been made to the bishop, reached the summit of the mountain in good time and in the identical spot where he had first seen her, stood the Blessed Virgin, in all the glory and majesty of her divine character awaiting his arrival. Juan in the most reverential manner conveyed to the glorious apparition his interview with the bishop and the demand made upon him for a sign. Congratulating Juan upon his faithfulness and obedience to her commands she ordered him to return the next day and his desire and that of the bishop should be complied with. Juan in the most thankful manner for the promised sign which should establish his veracity with the bishop, declared his intention to return at the time specified, and upon receiving the blessings of the Virgin departed for home much elated at the manner in which events were shaping themselves.

It was nearly night when Juan reached his simple hut where much to his astonishment and grief he learned that his uncle, Juan Bernadino upon whom he looked as a father had been stricken with the dreaded *cacolixtli*, a malignant disease peculiar to the region at certain seasons. Forgetful of all else but the sufferings of his relative he passed the whole of the next day (the 11th,) in administering such remedies as were known to the Indians, and in careful nursing, but without beneficial results. The morning of the 12th dawned but found the patient no better, in fact feeling that his end was near and too being a convert to the new religion, he implored Juan to hasten for a priest that he might receive the holy sacrament and extreme unction before he died.

While it was yet but early morning, and in obedience to his uncle's wishes Juan set out to seek a confessor, carefully avoiding the upper path across the mountain where he had seen the blessed vision, in fear of meeting it again and incurring the displeasure of the Virgin for his remission in not acceding to her command of the day before. So he followed a path much lower down which ran close to a spring, hoping thereby he might not be intercepted and chided for his shortcomings. What was his surprise on approaching the spring to see the Virgin in all her heavenly radiance waiting to meet him. The sight of the apparition filled Juan with fear and trembling as he thought of his dereliction, but as the Virgin greeted him with a benignant countenance his alarm somewhat subsided, but when asked: "Whither goest thou my son? What road is this thou has taken?" he became terribly confused and ashamed, not knowing what to say. Presently, however, he cast his eyes toward the Holy Lady, and observing the heavenly smile which lighted up her features he took courage and said: "Do not be offended Beloved Virgin, at what I am about to say to you;" *and after inquiring in relation to her health*, explained the cause of his absence of the day previous, and the mission upon which he was now bent, and hoped she would permit him to pass; that he would return soon and carry out her mandates. His story was listened to with the utmost suavity and gentleness, at the end of which the Virgin said to him: "Hear my son what I say. Do not allow yourself to be disturbed or afflicted by anything; neither fear infirmity, affliction, nor grief. Am not I, your mother, here? Are you not under my shield and protection? Do you need more? Give yourself neither trouble nor concern on account of the illness of your uncle, who will not die of this present malady, and, morover, rest satisfied that even at this instant he is perfectly cured."

Juan knowing now, that upon this, the third appearance of the beautiful vision, he was really in the awful presence of one of the Holy Family, and that it was not a phantasmagoria, the effect of a disturbed brain as had been suggested by the bishop, comforted himself with the thought, and abandoning all solicitude for the condition of his relative, asked for the promised "sign." The Virgin then directed him to "listen and carefully comply with her commands." She then told him to go to the place where she had first met him, and "cuting the flowers he would find there, to fill his blanket with them and return to her." Juan, in a spirit of perfect faith, hastened to obey, although he knew that nothing but thorns and brambles grew on the alkali ridge where he was directed to find flowers. Juan soon reached the spot where his eyes, days previously, had first feasted on the beautiful vision, and to his intense surprise, discovered a "bed of various budding flowers, odorous and yet wet with dew." He gazed long and fondly on the exquisitely formed and fragrant floral picture, and then suddenly remembering his mission, soon filled his blanket, as commanded, and carried them to the Virgin, whom he found waiting at the foot of a palm tree, called by the natives *Cuatzahautl*, and which bears beautiful white lily-shaped flowers. Juan presented her with the contents of his blanket in the most obsequious manner, and knelt at her feet in the attitude of prayer. The Lady, kindly smiling on Juan, took the offering in her hands, blessed the flowers and re-arranging them in the blanket, said to Juan: "This is the sign I wish you to take to the bishop, in order that he may build me a temple on this spot, and I command you, that you show no one what you have until you arrive in the presence of the bishop." The Virgin then blessed Juan who, with a happy heart, started on a run for the city and the palace of the bishop, for he knew now that he had tangible evidence to show that high functionary, and that his vision was realistic and that he would be believed. Juan soon reached the palace gate with his precious burden, and in an excited manner demanded to see the bishop at once, but the gate-keeper, knowing of his former visits and their bootlessness, declined to admit him. Juan, however, grew so impatient, and so enraged the man, that at last, after attempting to divest Juan of his precious gift of flowers, but observing that they were miraculously interwoven in his blanket, himself hastened to the bishop to inform him of the strange phenomenon, closely followed by Juan. The bishop, being informed of the remarkable occurrence, ordered Juan to come into his presence immediately. The Indian then unrolled his blanket before the eyes of the astonished prelate to exhibit the "sign," when lo! "the image of the Most Holy Virgin appeared painted upon the garment." As this most wonderful miracle greeted the bishop and his attendants, they all fell down and worshiped it with the greatest reverence. Poor Juan was as much surprised as any of them, he had no idea that his "sign" consisted of anything more than the loved flowers, and these, to him, were sufficient themselves, growing in winter and their radiant beauty, to satisfy him that he had really been given a sign. The bishop, after the proper adoration had been said to the wonderful picture, rose from his knees and reverently untied the knot that secured the blanket to Juan's neck, and taking it to his chapel, hung the "sacred cloth" behind the high altar, and again "gave thanks to God for so striking a miracle."

Juan during all that day was right royally entertained by the bishop, and the next day was ordered to show the exact place on the mountain where he had first seen the beautiful vision, and then the bishop was to order a temple to be erected to the memory of the Most Blessed and Holy Virgin, but upon reaching the summit, the Indian could not determine upon the exact locality, whereupon—as the legend declares—a stream gushed forth and "indicated it."

After this event, Juan begged permission of the bishop and the multitude of dignitaries that had accompanied him to the hill, to go and see his uncle whom he had left "nigh unto death." The worthy prelate consented and sent some of his retinue with Juan, and with orders if they found Juan Bernadino, his uncle, to bring him back with them.

As the crowd neared the village they met Bernadino perfectly recovered, and coming out to greet them. Juan then related his experience to his uncle, who declared that "on the self-same hour" on which the Most Holy Virgin announced his recovery, she had appeared to him, and not only cured him, but also had directed him to build a temple to her at Tepeyacac, where her image should be called "HOLY MARIA DE GUADALUPE."

In course of time, the celebrated church was built at Tepeyacac, and the alleged miraculous picture still hangs on its wall behind the great altar, as beautiful and as full of interest as when placed there nearly three hundred and fifty years ago.

It is sacredly guarded, and only a favored few are permitted to gaze upon its "exquisite sublimity." This honor was accorded to Mr. Seward during his visit to Mexico on his remarkable tour of the world, and in his book I believe he refers to it.

In one of the old churches at Santa Fe—the church of "Our Lady of Guadalupe"—may be seen a copy of the exquisite picture. The "Virgin" is represented—with a most decided caste of Indian features and complexion—standing upon the crescent moon, which in turn is supported by bodiless cherubs; her mantle is intensely blue, studded with stars and falls gracefully from her forehead to her feet.

In every house, in both Old and New Mexico, whether of the most abject or most opulent, an image of "Our Lady of Guadalupe" may be found, and her services are frequently called into requisition with much prayer and penance, as the tutelar saint of the country.

THE FIGHT ON LOWREY'S ISLAND (OPPOSITE LARNED), TWENTY YEARS AGO.

It was a magnificent September day in the early part of that month in the year 1860. The amber mist of the glorious Indian summer hung in light clouds over the rippling Pawnee, and the sheen of the noon-day sun on the Arkansas, made that silent stream where it broadens out lake-like, toward the now thriving little village of Garfield, sparkle and scintillate until it was painful for the eyes to rest upon it. The low group of sand-hills loomed up white and silvery, like the chalk cliffs of Dover, for in those days—before the march of immigration had wrought its remarkable changes in our climate—these sand-hills were bare, and for miles away the contour of the Arkansas could be traced by their conspicuous glare. The box elders and cottonwoods that fringed the tributaries to the river were rapidly donning their Autumn dress of russet, and the mirage had already in the early mornings commenced its weird and fantastic play with the landscape.

Under the shadow of the bluff where Larned now reposes so picturesquely, hundreds of buffaloes were grazing, and on the plateau above the crest of the hill, where Mayor Sunderland's handsome residence overlooks the town and the broad valley, a few sentinel antelopes were guarding their charge, now quietly ruminating their morning's meal in the ravines running toward the river.

Near where Brown's grove is located, under the grateful shade of the thickest clumps of timber, about forty wigwams were irregularly scattered, and on the hills a herd of two or three hundred ponies were lazily feeding, guarded by half a dozen superannuated squaws, while a troop of dusky little children were chasing the yellow butterflies from the now dried and dying sun-flower stalks that so conspicuously marked the broad trail to the river. This beautiful spot had been selected by Black Kettle, chief of the Cheyennes, for his winter camp, to which only a few weeks previously he had moved from the Canadian, and settled with his band to hunt on the Arkansas Bottom, and watch his enemies, the Pawnees, who claimed the same ground, and where year after year the most sanguinary battles between the two tribes had been fought. Apart from the remainder of the wigwams, and near the edge of the stream was the magnificent lodge of Yellow Buffalo, the war chief of the Cheyennes. This lodge was formed of beautifully porcupined and beaded robes, and its interior was *graced* with a long row of scalps—the trophies of his fame as a great warrior.

On the morning of the date mentioned, I had reached the Arkanses at a point a few miles east of the mouth of the Pawnee, on my way to Ft. Larned from my ranch on Sharp's Creek, (now in McPherson county,) and when near where Larned stands I noticed a large body of Indians in a stooping attitude, as though hunting for something, and I supposed them to be some of my Kiowa friends on the trail of an enemy. I spurred my horse and rode toward them, when suddenly they dropped in the grass, which convinced me of the error of my first supposition. I was well acquainted at that time with nearly all the tribes on the plains, and particularly with those who would probably be in that vicinity then, and with a fair knowledge of the Indian character I readily concluded that my covey in the grass were a band of "dog soldiers," of some tribe, either on the war path against some of the other tribes that roamed in the valley of the Arkansas, or were a party to steal horses; in either event I had little to fear, as the report of a gun would be the last thing they would care to hear just then.

So I rode on, and when within a hundred yards or so of the party, one rose, and holding both hands up with palms to the front, in his own dialect called my name. I felt considerably relieved for I found myself among thirty-two Pawnees, who, as I first supposed, were there to steal horses from the Cheyennes and Kiowas. On learning this fact, I told them that a few miles back on the trail, I had seen a large number of Indians on the high prairie scattered out as if surrounding buffalo, or elk, but that I had seen no game, and now I knew their presence was known to the Arkansas tribes, and that there were so many of these wild Indians the few Pawnees would all be killed if found.

They then told me they wanted to reach the island in the

river, and there could fight all the *Ingins* that dare to come, and if they got to the island before the wild Indians found them, I must go to them and tell them that they were there, and myself come and see the fight. That if I staid on my horse, either on the east or west side of the island, or on the hill on the northwest, I could see it all and be safe from their bullets; and if they all got killed I should tell their people how grandly and bravely they died.

I left them and went on toward the fort, and when within three miles of it, met "Yellow Buffalo" with two hundred of his warriors, their war-paint on and beating their drums furiously.

"Yellow Buffalo" was then about thirty years old, and as magnificent a looking Indian as I ever saw. I delivered my message from the Pawnees to him, immediately upon which the two hundred warriors raised the war-cry, which echoed and reverberated in all the splendor of its savage grandeur over the prairie, and which none but those who have heard it under such circumstances can appreciate.

Stung to the heart by my message of defiance, "Yellow Buffalo" appeared the true savage that he really was, all the ferocity of his wild nature glaring in his eyes as he thought of the deep wrongs done to his tribe by the "dogs of Pawnees!" as he called them, and appealing to his men " that now was the time presented to them, to not only reap an adequate revenge, but add lasting laurels to their wreaths as brave and skillful warriors," he again gave the signal for another challenging yell, and pointed to the hiding place of his enemies down the river with an air of derision.

We were a short distance south of the old Santa Fe trail, and ordering his band to turn nearly due south, we loped off in the direction of the island. As we neared the river bank, we saw the last of the Pawnees—who had been watching our approach—plunge into the stream and reach the island in safety, as our advance halted on the spot where now rests the north end of the Larned bridge. It was about two o'clock in the afternoon, the Cheyennes dismounted, and every tenth man went to the rear to hold the horses and guard them from a possible flank movement on the part of the Pawnees. I was honored by "Yellow Buffalo" with the privilege of taking care of my own horse—which, I am happy to say, I did from a position on the south end of the hill west of the town, and as near the river as was prudent for a non-combatant. Nearly all the Cheyennes were armed with muzzle-loading rifles, and a third of them had Colt's large army revolvers. At the command of their chief, "Yellow Buffalo" the Cheyennes formed a line of battle, which seemed to extend up and down the river the whole length of the island, while five or six of them acted as flankers. During this disposition of the forces, not a Pawnee was to be seen.

In those days the island was covered only with dwarf willows, the Box-Elders which have, within the past few years, graced it, were then unknown, and instead of the parklike and arborescent form it assumes to-day, it was merely a rather excellent hiding place for the savage, or a home for the fragrant skunk. The thick willows concealed the watchful Pawnees, who were rather better armed than the Cheyennes, in consequence of the former living in close communion with the settlements. They each had a Spencer carbine— then the arm *par-excellence* of the frontier—and two revolvers either army or navy pattern, besides their bows, and quivers well filled with arrows. When all was in readiness, and "Yellow Buffalo" had made a proper disposition of his forces, he gave the order to charge! Upon hearing his clear voice ring across the prairie, his warriors responded with a most unearthly yell that seemed to shake even the eternal dunes of sand on the opposite side of the river, and then rushed pell-mell into the Arkansas. The water was waist high, and as they advanced they kept up their infernal whoop until they reached within ten feet of the island, when like a flash of light from a clear sky came a sheet of flame from the edge of the willows, which was promptly responded to by the braves in the water.

In an instant, however, as much to my surprise as to their enemies, the Pawnees delivered from their ranks another volley followed immediately by the quick sharp crack of their revolvers, which seemed completely to overwhelm and discomfort the Cheyennes, all of whom beat a hasty retreat to the main land. Their war-whoop ceased the instant the Cheyennes commenced their backward march, and in a moment some twenty of the Pawnees appeared above the willows, and kept up a well directed fire on their foes until the latter reached the bank of the river.

In this single charge of the Cheyennes, thirteen were killed outright and twenty-three wounded, which evinced a coolness and deliberation on the part of the Pawnees not excelled by the best organized troops. The Cheyennes in their charge showed their characteristic recklessness and daring, which, however, counted for nothing in results, as all the shots were carried clear over the heads of the Pawnees who were concealed by the friendly willows.

While the main body of the Pawnees were keeping up their almost incessant fire upon the retreating Cheyennes, three or four others arose at opposite ends of the Island, and opened with some well delivered shots with their carbines at the Cheyenne flankers, so that the whole number became demoralized, and "Yellow Buffalo," with all his painted warriors, fled as far back as to where the Presbyterian church now stands on Main street, and held a council. "Yellow Buffalo" then got on his horse and rode up the hill to me, and asked me "how many Pawnees I had seen."

I told him I did not count them, but to the best of my judgment there were not more than thirty-five, but the way they spoke of reaching the island as a place of safety, they might have had reference to more men there, than to the strength of their medicine.

He answered despondingly, "they must have more than

two hundred from the number of shots fired, and the way they were scattered along the bank."

"Yellow Buffalo" then dispatched a messenger for reinforcements, and in about an hour they arrived from the south of the river to the number of four or five hundred, and upon their joining the others, "Yellow Buffalo" made the same disposition of his now augmented forces as he had with his original army, and then turned his command over to "Black Kettle," who had come on the ground.

"Black Kettle kept his Indians in close order, and when they reached within shooting distance of the island, the Pawnees opened upon them with a terrible volley, and the most deafening and diabolical yells, and kept it up for at least ten minutes. The poor Cheyennes returned the fire as best they could, but invariably overshot the Pawnees whom they could not see, so closely were they hidden by the willows.

In the wild firing, many bullets passed over my head, and I made a masterly strategic movement to the east of the town, and again escaped danger. Meanwhile, "Black Kettle, as well as myself, ingloriously retreated from whence we came, and then "Yellow Buffalo" felt himself no more disgraced than the "head war chief" and *his* chosen warriors. Thus ended this rather remarkable fight. I never could learn definitely how many of the Cheyennes were killed or wounded in the second charge—the Pawnees told me they were double the number of the first charge, but coming as it did from the victors, I always made a reasonable allowance for possible exaggeration. The Cheyennes utterly refused to tell me the number of their loss, but I saw the wounded that night, and helped dress most of their wounds. There were twenty-eight in "Black Kettle's" camp alone. He admitted no deaths, but I saw them pack more than thirty out of the river, and the Pawnees took five scalps, which I saw them go and procure about twenty minutes after the second charge. On my return from the Fort next day with my mail, the Cheyennes informed me that these same Pawnees charged through the guards and actually drove off about two hundred of the Cheyennes' ponies.

The Pawnees assured me that they had but forty warriors all told, and they they lost in killed and wounded but two. The Cheyennes stated, however, that they "found five graves in the sand-hills under the edge of the water, which they exhumed and left the bodies to rot, and the bones to bleach on the prairie like a coyote."

The Cheyennes would never refer to the fight of their own accord, and only spoke of it with the greatest reluctance when the subject was forced upon them.

A LEGEND OF PAWNEE ROCK;

OR,

HOW THE LIFE OF AN OLD TRAPPER WAS SAVED BY A BIRD.

The thinly scattered, and now almost obliterated trails leading in every direction away from Pawnee Rock, have a fearful record of desperate adventures and journeys that often ended there with tragic death, and volumes could be written were it possible to gather the materials floating in legendary form among the old trappers, but these are, unfortunately, rapidly passing away, and much that would be full of interest must be irrevocably lost.

The hardy trappers in the early days of the "Great Central Plains," isolated themselves in the vast solitudes of the interior of the continent, and only made their visits to the small trading stations on the "River," as the Missouri was called—like those attributed to angels—"few and far between."

Many of them indulged in the most extravagant stories and strange adventures, occasionally bordering on the supernatural, all of which was usually unsuspiciously swallowed by the ignorant and gaping crowd of listeners who were ready to believe anything of the mysteries beyond the settlements.

At that time the whole region stretching from the Missouri to the Mountains was an unexplored wilderness, excepting a narrow belt contiguous to the river—a sort of *terra incognita* in fact, whose woods and streams abounded in remarkably fertile themes for the play of the wildest imagination.

The trade with New Mexico via the Plains was inaugurated in 1823, at which date the first train of wagons that ever traveled in that direction, started from Boonville, Missouri. Their route was directly up the valley of the Arkansas to Pawnee Rock, and for fifty years—until the advent of the railroad in this portion of Kansas in 1873—the trail of the freighters passed within a hundred rods of the Rock.

For years, the idea of the possibility of the settlement of that great inter-continental tract never entered the minds of even the most sanguine believer in the future of that portion of our domain—it was a desert to all intents and purposes, according to the early geographers, and a desert it was to remain.

But the extension of our vast railway system beyond the Mississippi forever determined the question of the settlement of the plains—which in 1872 reached as far as Pawnee Rock. The "desert" has disappeared, and in its place has risen one grand picture of fertility and happy homes.

As has been referred to in "How Pawnee Rock was Named," the remains of those who met their death in the vicinity of the Rock are frequently ploughed up in the spring and fall. These frequent graves are a source of curiosity and a matter of speculation and gossip to those who have recently moved here—whose homes have ever been in the far-back civilization of the crowded East, and who are necessarily ignorant of the traditions and history of that portion of the plains on which they have settled. Only little more than a year ago one of these new-comers, a well-to-do farmer, living a few miles west of Larned on Pawnee Bottom, having observed in one of his fields a singular depression, remarkably resembling an old grave, such as is frequently found in venerable church yards, he determined to dig down and see if there was any special cause for the strange indentation on his land.

At a couple of feet below the surface he discovered several flat pieces of stone, on one of which the words: "Washington" and "J. Hildreth" were rudely cut, also a line separating them, and underneath the date: "December 10" and "J. M., 1850." On another was carved the name "J. H. Shell," and other characters that could not be deciphered. On a third stone were the initials "H. R., 1847," underneath this was plainly cut "J. R. Boyd," and still beneath this "J. R. Pring." At the very bottom of the excavation were found the lower portion of the skull, one or two ribs, and one of the bones of the leg of a human being. The piece of skull was found near the center of the grave, for such it certainly was. Who were the parties whose names were thus strangely handed down on those rude fragments of stone? Who had been buried there, and why could only the under portion of the skull of one be found? Was he an emigrant crossing the plains for far-off Oregon, or the rich placers of

California, and, stricken by disease, kindly buried there on the lone prairie by his companions? Or was he a hunter, and in fierce combat with the Indians sent by the murderous scalping knife to his untimely grave? These were the character of the questions asked of each other in the little settlement last summer, when the little grave was opened.

At any rate some one died there, the knowledge of whose existence has only thus curiously come to light years after he had almost crumbled into dust.

A story strange and romantic enough for the most sensational minds is frequently woven by the brains of our novelists out of as few and meager facts as are found in the above simple discovery of a few roughly cut stones and crumbling bones, and an imaginative writer could easily weave one out of these, but such is not my purpose.

At the time of the discovery of this old grave I consulted my book of notes and memoranda taken hurriedly at intervals on the plains for half a life-time, to see if I could find in the legends and anecdotes I have picked up from time to time, anything that would solve the mystery attached to that quiet prairie grave and its contents. I succeeded in finding among my mass of manuscript a crude and unadorned little sketch, gleaned from an old trapper some twelve years since, that partially clears up the secret, and throws a ray of light upon the death of him whose bones have been waiting Christian burial, on the river bottom, a few miles from Pawnee Rock, these thirty years. A conversation and interchange of notes on the subject with Col. A. G. Boone* the past winter, confirms the probability of the truth of the story as given to me so many years ago.

Of course every one who has lived or traveled on the plains during the last quarter of a century, remembers Uncle John Smith.† He was an old trapper and guide—had been among the Indians for more than forty years—and figured only a little less conspicuously in the history of the Far West than Kit Carson, Maxwell and other sons of the border.

Old Uncle John was a character in his way, and as full of cranks and superstitions as a Congo negro. I am sorry to observe, too, that his reputation for unexaggerated and orthodox truth was not as immaculate as he of the cherry tree notoriety, and therefore I should have taken his statement, which is the subject of this sketch, *cum grano salis*, had it not been confirmed by that eloquent old gentleman, Col. Boone.

"Uncle John" was a perfect encyclopedia of plains' lore, and acquainted with every foot of country beyond the Missouri, or as he used to express it, "had slept under every cottonwood and drank out of every spring from the mouth of the Yellowstone to the Red river of the South."

I was camping with the old man in November, 1868, on

---

*Col. A. G. Boone is still hale and vigorous, and as wiry as his celebrated grandfather, the pioneer hero of Kentucky. He is a splendid specimen of a well-preserved frontiersman, possessing a knowledge of the Indian in all his varied situations not excelled by any one, and enjoys the confidence of nearly all the tribes and every old white hunter on the plains. H. I.

†He died in 1873, and is buried among the Cheyennes, who adopted him more than forty years ago.

the bank of the Wachita, only a short time after Custer's memorable fight with Black Kettle, waiting with a train of supplies for the troops who had been ordered to rendezvous by General Sheridan at that point. We had been living almost exclusively on wild turkey for the weary fourteen days of our sojourn on that historic creek, and were heartily tired of them. One evening some of our party had succeeded in bagging a few quails, and when the announcement was made of a prospective change of diet, it was received with evident satisfaction. Late in the evening when my cook brought the delicious little birds, beautifully spitted, on peeled willow twigs, into my tent, and passed one to "Uncle John" in his turn, he refused. Said he, "Boys, I don't eat no quail."

All the rest of us were completely surprised, for "Uncle John" was considerable of a gourmand and prided himself upon the "faculty," as he termed it, of being able to eat anything, from a piece of jerked buffalo hide to the juiciest young antelope steak.

I said: "'Uncle John,' these birds are magnificently broiled; you are making a mistake, old man; to-morrow we must leave here, and as we are going straight away from the buffalo country, we don't know when we shall strike fresh meat again. You had better try one.

"Boys," said he, "I don't tech quail; I hain't teched one for more nor twenty years. One of the little cusses saved my live once, and I swore right thar and then that I would starve fust, and I've kept that oath, though I've seen the time I could a killed 'em with my quirt, when all I had to chaw on for four days was the soles of a greasy old moccasin."

Of course our whole party was eager to know how the life of the old trapper had been saved by a little bird, and in a few moments every man in camp gathered around the dying embers of the cook's fire to listen to "Uncle John's" story. I filled up the old man's pipe with some of my best "Lone Jack," lighted it, took a pull, Indian fashion, and passed it to him. He loved good tobacco, and was always more communicative when seated around the camp-fire, half-hidden in a cloud of smoke. One of the men threw a chunk of dry cottonwood on the coals, and as the flames began to lick up the shaggy bark, casting a pleasant shimmer on the old guide's face, he took a vigorous pull at his pipe and commenced.

"Well, boys, it's a good many years ago—in June, if I don't disremember—1847. We was a coming in from way up in "Cache le Poudre," and from Yellowstone Lake, whar we'd been a trapping for two seasons. We was a working our way slowly back to Independence, Missouri, where we was a going to get a new outfit. Let's see—there was me, and a man by the name of Boyd, and Lew Thorp—Lew was a working for Colonel Boone at the time—and two more men whose names I disremember now, and a nigger wench we had for a cook. We had mighty good luck, and had a big pile of skins; and the Indians never troubled us till we got down on Pawnee Bottom, this side of Pawnee Rock. We all of us had mighty good ponies, but Thorp had a team and wagon, which he was driving for Colonel Boone.

"We had went into camp on Pawnee Bottom airly in the afternoon, and I told the boys to look out for Indians—for I knowed ef we was to have any trouble with them it would be somewhere in that vicinity. But we didn't see a darned redskin that night, nor the sign of one.

"The wolves howled considerable, and cum pretty close to the fire after the bacon rinds we'd throwed away after supper.

"You see the buffalo was scurse right thar then—it was the wrong time o'year. They generally don't get down onto the Arkansas till about September, and when ther'e scurse, the wolves and coyotes are mighty sassy, and will steal a piece of bacon rind right out of the pan, if you don't watch 'em. So we picketed our ponies a little closer, before we turned in and we all went to sleep except one, who sort o'keep watch on the stock.

"I was out o' my blankets mighty airly next morning, for I was kind o' suspicious. I could always tell when Indians was prowling around, and I had a sort of present'ment something was going to happen—I didn't like the way the coyotes kept yelling—so I rested kind o' oneasy like, and was out among the ponies by the first streak o' daylight.

"About the time I could fairly see things, I discovered three or four buffalo grazing off on the creek bottom, about a half mile away, and I started for my rifle, thinking I would examine her, and after we'd had breakfast go out and blow one of the critters in.

"Pretty soon I seed Thorp and Boyd crawl out o' their blankets, too, and I called their attention to the buffalo, which was still feeding undisturbed.

"We'd been kind o' scurse of fresh meat for a couple of weeks—ever since we left the Platte, except a jack-rabbit or cottontail, and I knowed the boys would be wanting to get a quarter or two of a good fat cow, if we could find one in the herd so that was the reason I pointed 'em out to 'em.

"The dew—you see—was mighty heavy, and the grass in the bottom was as wet as if it had been raining for a month, and I didn't care to go down whar the buffalo was just then —I knowed we had plenty of time and as soon as the sun was up it would dry right off. So I got onto one of the ponies and led the others down to the spring near camp to water them while the wench was a getting breakfast, and some o' the rest o' the outfit was a fixin the saddles and greasing the wagon.

"Just as I was coming back—it had growed quite light then—I seed Boyd and Thorp start out from camp with their rifles and make for the buffalo, so I picketed the ponies, gets my rifle and starts off too.

"By the time I'd reached the edge of the bottom, Thorp and Boyd was a crawling up onto a young bull way off to the right, and I lit out for a fat cow I seen bunched up with the rest of the herd on the left.

"The grass was mighty tall on some parts of the Arkansas bottom in them days, and I got within easy shooting range without the herd seeing me.

"The buffalo was now between me and Thorp and Boyd, and they was further from camp. I could see them over the top of the grass kind o' edging up to the bull, and I kept a crawling on my hands and knees toward the cow, and when I got about a hundred and fifty yards of her, I pulled up my rifle and drawed a bead.

"Just as I was running my eye along the bar'l a darned little quail flew right out from under my feet and lit exactly on my front sight and of course cut off my aim—we didn't shoot reckless in those days; every shot had to tell, or a man was the laughing stock for a month if he missed his game.

"I shook the little critter off and brought up my rifle again when durn my skin if the bird didn't lite right onto the same place; at the same time my eyes growed kind o' hazy like and in a minute I didn't know nothing.

"When I come to the quail was gone, I heerd a couple of rifle shots, and right in front of where the bull had stood and close to Thorp and Boyd, half a dozen Indians jumped up out o' the tall grass and firing into the two men, killed Thorp instantly and wounded Boyd

"He and me got to camp—keeping off the Indians who knowed I was loaded—when we, with the rest of the outfit, drove the red devils away.

"They was Apaches, and the fellow that shot Thorp was a half breed nigger and Apache. He scalped Thorp and carried off the *whole upper part of his skull* with it. He got Thorp's rifle and bullet pouch too, and his knife.*

"We buried Thorp in the bottom here, and some of the party cut their names on the stones that they covered his body up with, to keep the coyotes from eating up his bones.

"Boyd got onto the river with us all right, and I never heerd of him after we separated at Booneville. We pulled out soon after the Indians left, but we didn't get no buffalo meat.

"You see boys, if I'd a fired into that cow the devils would a had me before I could a got a patch on my ball—didn't have no breech-loaders in them days, and it took as much judgment to know how to load a rifle properly as it did to shoot it.

"Them Indians knowed all that—they knowed I hadn't fired, so they kept 'a respectable distance. I would a fired but the quail saved my life by interfering with my sight—and that's the reason I don't eat no quail—I hain't superstitious, but I don't believe they was meant to be eat."

Uncle John stuck to his text, I believe, until he died, and you could never disabuse his mind of the idea that the quail lighting on his rifle was not a special interposition of Providence.

---

*Col. A. G. Boone confirms all this, and got back the articles a short time afterward from the Chief of the Apaches.

ANOTHER LEGEND OF PAWNEE ROCK.

"Pawnee Rock" has probably been the scene of a hundred fights, and a volume could be written in relation to it. Kit Carson, one night some fifteen years ago, when he, Jack Henderson, Lucien B. Maxwell, a couple of Apache Indians and myself, were camped half way up the rugged sides of "Old Baldy," in the "Raton Range," told in his peculiarly expressive way, among other border reminiscences, the following little story, the incidents of which occurred long years ago.

The night was cold, although midsummer, and we were huddled around a little fire of pine knots more than eight thousand feet above the level of the sea, close to the snow limit. We had left Maxwell's early in the morning to trace a quartz lead that cropped out near the mouth of the copper mine worked by him, and night overtook us many miles from the ranch, so we concluded to remain on the mountain until daylight. We had no blankets, and, of course, had to sit up through the long hours, and as it was terribly cold, made a fire, filled our pipes, and spun yarns to keep awake. Our lunch that we had brought was eaten up about noon, so we were supperless as well, but a swift, cold mountain stream ran close to our little camp and we took a swallow of that occasionally, which served the place of a meal.

Kit (the General, as every one called him) was in a good humor for talking, and we naturally took advantage of this to draw him out, for usually he was the most reticent of men in relation to his own exploits. The night was pretty dark—there was no moon—and our fire of dry knots blazed up beautifully every time the two Indians—whom we had appointed to this special duty—threw a fresh armful on. The flames cast their weird and fanciful shadows on the side of the mountain, and contrasted curiously with the inky blackness all around below us, while far above could be seen the dim outline of "Old Baldy's" scarred and weather-beaten crest, piled crag upon crag until they seemed to touch the star-lit sky.

For an hour or two the conversation was confined to the probabilities of gold being found in paying quantities in the mountains and gulches of the range, and when the interest on that subject flagged, Maxwell having made a casual remark in relation to some peak near by, just discernable in the darkness, and connecting the locality with some trouble he had had ten or a dozen years before with the Indians, opened Kit Carson's mouth, and he said he remembered one of the "worst difficults" a man ever got into, so he made a fresh corn shuck cigarette and told us the following about Pawnee Rock, which he said had been written up years ago, and that he had á paper containing it, (which he afterward gave me,) and which, with what Kit related orally that night, is here presented:

"It was old Jim Gibson—poor fellow he went under in a fight with the Utes over twenty years ago, and his bones are bleaching somewhere in the dark cañons of the Range, or on the slopes of the Spanish Peaks. He used to tell of a scrimmage he and another fellow had on the Arkansas with the Kiowas in 1836.

"Jim and his pardner, Bill something or other, I disremember his name now, had been trapping up in the Powder River country during the winter with unusual good luck—the beaver was mighty thick in the whole Yellowstone region in them days, and Jim and Bill got an early start on their journey for the River that spring—you see they expected to sell their truck in Weston, Missouri, which was the principal trading point on the river then. They walked the whole distance—over fifteen hundred miles—driving three good mules before them, on which their plunder was packed, and they got along well enough until they struck the Arkansas at Pawnee Rock. Here they met a war-party of about sixty Kiowas, who treed them on the Rock. Jim and Bill were notoriously brave, and both dead shots. Before they reached the Rock, to which they were driven, they killed ten of the Kiowas, and had not received a scratch. They had plenty of powder and a pouch full of bullets each. They also had a couple of jack-rabbits for food in case of a siege, and the perpendicular walls of the Rock made them a natural fortification—an almost impregnable one.*

"They succeeded in securely picketing their animals on the west side of the Rock where they could protect them by their unerring rifles—but the story of the fight must be told in Jim's own way—he was a pretty well educated fellow, had been to college, I believe, in his younger days, lost the gal he was going to marry, or had some bad luck or other, and took to the prairies when he was about twenty. I will try to tell it as nearly as he did as possible.

"After the durned red cusses had treed us, they picked up their dead and packed them to their camp at the mouth of the creek a little piece off. In a few moments back they all came mounted, with all their fixings and war paint on. Then they commenced to circle around us, coming closer, Indian fashion, every time, till they got within easy rifle range, when they slung themselves on the fore side of their ponies, and, in that position, opened on us. Their arrows fell like a hail storm around us for a few moments, but, as good luck would have it, none of them struck. I was afraid they would, first of all, attempt to kill our mules; but I suppose they thought they had the dead wood on us, and the mules would come mighty handy for their own use after our scalps were dangling at their belts. But we were taking in

---
*Pawnee Rock has, through the agency of man, changed much since the advent of the railroad. Its once lofty summit has been stripped and the stone used for all sorts of purposes by the farmers and the road, so that now it is only a comparatively low mound.—H. I.

all the chances—Bill kept his eyes skinned, and whenever he saw a stray leg or head he drew a bead on it, and thug, over tumbled its owner every time, with a yell of rage.

"Whenever they attempted to carry off their dead that was the moment we took the advantage, and we poured it into them as soon as they rallied for that purpose with telling effect. We wasted no shots; we had now only about forty bullets between us, and the miserable cusses seemed thick as ever.

"The sun was nearly down by this time, and at dark they did not seem anxious to renew the fight that night, but I could see their mounted patrols at a respectable distance on every side watching to prevent our escape. I took advantage of the darkness to go down and get a few buffalo chips to cook our supper, for we were mighty hungry, and to change the animals to where they could get a little more grass, though for that matter it was nearly up to a man's head all over the bottom.

"I got back to our camp on top without any trouble, when we made a little fire and cooked a rabbit. We had to go without water and so did the animals, but we did not mind the want of it so much ourselves, but pitied the mules that had none since we broke camp in the morning. It was no use to worry about it though; the nearest water was in the spring at the Indian camp, and it would be certain death to attempt to get there without their seeing us.

"I was afraid the red devils would fire the prairie in the

morning, and endeavor to smoke or burn us out. The grass was just in a condition to make a lively blaze, and we might escape the flames and we might not.

"We watched with eager eyes for the first gray streaks of dawn that would usher in another day—perhaps the last for us.

"The next morning's sun had scarcely peeped above the horizon, when, with an infernal yell the Indians broke for the Rock, and we knew some new project had entered their heads.

"The wind was springing up pretty fresh, and nature seemed to conspire with the red devils if they really meant to burn us out, and I had no doubt now from their movements that was what they intended.

"The darned cusses kept at such a respectable distance from our rifles that it chafed us to know that we could not stop the infernal throats of some of them with our bullets, but we had to choke our rage and watch events closely.

"I took occasion during the lull in hostilities to crawl down to where the mules were and shift them to the east side of the "Rock," where the wall was the highest, so that the flame and smoke might possibly pass by them without so much danger as on the exposed other side.

"I succeeded in doing this, and also in tearing the grass away for several yards around the animals, and was just starting back when Bill called out, "Damn 'em, they've fired the prairie.'

"I reached the top of the Rock in a moment, and took in at a glance what was coming.

"The spectacle for a short interval was indescribably grand. The sun was shining with all the power of its rays on the huge clouds of smoke as it rolled down from the north, tinting it with glorious a crimson. I had barely time to get under the shelter of a projecting point of the Rock when the wind and smoke swept down to the ground, and instantly we were enveloped in the darkness of midnight.

"We could not discern a single object; neither Indians, horses, the prairie, or sun—and what a terrible wind! I have never experienced its equal in violence since.

"We stood breathless, and clinging to the projection of our little mass of rock did not realize the fire was so near, until we were struck in the face by the burning buffalo-chips that were carried toward us with the rapidity of the wind.

"I was really scared; it seemed as if we must suffocate. But we were saved miraculously; the sheet of flame passed us twenty yards away, as the wind fortunately shifted the moment the fire reached the foot of the Rock. Yet the darkness was so perfect that we did not see the flame; we only knew that we were safe as the clear sky greeted us behind the dense cloud of smoke.

"Two of the Indians and their horses were caught in their own trap, and perished miserably. They had attempted to reach the east side of the Rock where the mules were, either to cut them loose or to crawl up on us while bewildered in the smoke if we escaped death. But they had proceeded only a few rods on their little expedition when the terrible darkness of the smoke-cloud overtook them.

"All the game on the prairie which the fire swept over was killed, too. Only a few buffaloes were visible in that region before the fire, but even they were killed.

"The path of this horrible passage of flames, as we found out afterward, was marked all along with the crisp and blackened carcasses of wolves, coyotes, turkeys, grouse, and every variety of small birds. Indeed, it seemed as if no living thing it met had escaped its fury.

"The fire assumed such gigantic proportions and moved with such rapidity before the terrible wind, that even the Arkansas river did not check its path for a moment, but we watched it carried across as readily as if it had not been in the way.

"This fearful prairie-fire traveled at the rate of eight miles in fifteen minutes, and was probably the most violent in its features that ever visited that country. It was the most sublime picture I ever looked upon, and for a moment made us forget our perilous position.

"My first thought after the danger from the fire had passed was of the poor mules, I crawled down to where they were and found them badly singed, but not seriously hurt. I thought 'so far so good;' our mules and traps were all right, and we were all right, so we took fresh courage and began to think we should get out of the nasty scrape in some way or other.

"In the mean time the Indians, with the exception of four or five left to guard the Rock so we could not escape, had gone back to their camp on the creek, and were evidently concocting some new stratagem to capture or kill us.

"We waited patiently two or three hours for the development of events, snatching a little sleep by turns until the sun was about four hours high, when the Indians commenced their infernal howling again, and we knew they had hit upon something, so we were on the alert in a moment to discover it and eucher them if possible.

"The devils this time had tied all their horses together, covered them with branches of trees that they had cut on the creek, packed all the lodge-skins on these, and then driving the living breast-works before them toward us, themselves followed close behind on foot.

"They kept moving slowly but surely in the direction of the 'Rock,' and matters began to look serious for us once more.

"Bill put his hand in mine, and said, 'Jim, now by G—d we got to fight, we haint done nothing yit; this means business.'

"I said 'you're right, Bill, old fellow; but they can't get us alive. Our plan is to kill their ponies, and make the cusses halt.'

"As I spoke, Bill—who was one of the best shots on

the plains—kind 'o threw his eye carelessly along the bar'l of his rifle, and one of the ponies tumbled over on the blackened sod. One of the Indians ran out to cut him loose, as I expected, and I took him clean off his feet without a groan. Quicker than it takes me to tell it, we had stretched out twelve of them on the prairie, and we made it so hot for them that they got out of range, and were apparently holding a council of war. We kept watching the devils' movements, for we knew they would soon be up to some confounded trick

"The others did not make their appearance immediately from behind their moving breast-works, so we both fired two shots apiece into the horses, killing three of them, and throwing the whole outfit into confusion.

"We soon stopped their little plan, and they had now only the dead bodies of the ponies we had killed to protect them, for the others had broken loose and stampeded off to camp. It was getting pretty hot for Mr. Indian now, who was on foot, and in easy range of our rifles. We cleaned out one or two more while they were gradually pulling themselves out of range, when of course, we had to stop firing. The Indians started off to their camp again and during the lull in hostilities took an account of stock, we found we had used up all our ammunition except three or four loads, and despair seemed to hover over us once more.

"In a few moments we were surprised to see one of the warriors come out alone from the camp, and tearing off a piece of his white blanket, boldly walked toward the ' Rock.' Coming up within hearing, he asked if we would have a talk with him. We told him yes, but did not look for any good results from it. We could not expect anything less than torture if we allowed ourselves to be taken alive, so we determined not to be caught in any trap.

"We knew we had done them too much damage to expect any mercy, so we prepared to die in the fight, if we must die. We beckoned the young buck nearer and listened to what he had to communicate. He said they were part of White Buffalo's band of Kiowas, that the war chief who was here with them was O-ton-son-e-var, (a herd of buffaloes), and that he wanted us to come to the camp—that we were ' heap brave '—we should be kindly treated, and that the tribe would adopt us. They were on their way to the Sioux country north of the Platte—that they were going there to steal horses from the Sioux. They expected a fight and wanted us to help them. Bill and myself knew the darned Indians too well to swallow their chaff, so we both told him we could not think of accepting their terms—that we were on our way to the Missouri, and meant to go there or die in the attempt—that we did not fear them, the white man's God would take care of us, and that if that was all they had to talk about he could go back, and tell his party they could commence the fight again as soon as they pleased.

" He started back, and before he had reached the creek

they came out and met him, had a confab, and then began the attack on us at once.

"We made each of our four loads tell, when we stood at bay, almost helpless, and defenseless; we were at the mercy of the savages, and they understood our situation as quickly as ourselves.

"We were now thrown upon our last resource—the boys play of throwing stones. As long as we could find detached pieces of the rock they did not dare to make an assault, and while we were still wondering what next, the white flag appeared again and demanded another talk. We knew that now we had to come to terms, and made up our minds to accept anything that savored of reason, and our life, trusting to the future to escape if they kept us as prisoners.

"'The Kiowas are not coyotes, and they know brave men,' said the Indian; 'we will not kill you, though the prairie grass is red with the blood of our warriors that have died by your hands. We will give you a chance for your lives, and let you prove that the Great Spirit of the white man is powerful, and can save you.'

"'Behold!' said the Indian, pointing with an arrow to a solitary cottonwood on the banks of the Arkansas, a mile or more away. 'You must go there, and one of you shall run the knife-gauntlet from that tree two hundred steps of the chief out toward the prairie. If the one who runs escapes, both are free, for the Great Spirit has willed it.

O-ton-son-e-var* has said it, and the words of the Kiowa are true."

"'When must the trial take place,' said I.

"'When the sun begins to shine upon the western edge of the Rock,' replied the Indian.

"'Say to your chief we accept the challenge and I will be ready,' said Bill, motioning the young warrior away. 'I am sure I can win,' said he, 'and can save both our lives. O-ton-son-e-var will keep his word, I know him.'

"'Bill,' said I, 'I shall run that race, not you;' and taking him by the hand, I told him that if he saw I was going to fail, to watch his chance, and in the excitement of the moment mount one of their horses, and fly toward Bent's Fort; he could escape, he was young—it made no difference with me—my life was not worth much, but he had all before him.'

"'No,' replied Bill, my heart is set on this; I traveled the same race once before when the Apaches got me, and their knives never struck me once. I ask this favor as my life for I have a preseentiment that it is only I that can win. I know how to get every advantage of them. So say 'no more.'

"The sun had scarcely gilded the dark line of rock that juts out boldly toward the western horizon, before all the warriors, with O-ton-son-e-var at their head, marched silently toward the tree and beckoned us to come.

---

* O-ton-son-e-var in fact was not a Kiowa but a Cheyenne. He died of cholera on the head-waters of the Smoky Hill in 1849.—H. I.

"Quickly we were on the prairie beside them, when they opened a space, and we walked in their center without exchanging a word. There were only thirty left of that band of sixty proud warriors who had commenced the attack on us the day before, and I could see by the scowls with which they regarded us, and the convulsive clutching at their knives by the younger ones, it was only the presence and power of O-ton-son-e-var that prevented them from taking summary vengeance upon us.

"As soon as we reached the tree, O-ton-son-e-var paced the two hundred steps, and arranged his warriors on either side, who in a moment stripped themselves to the waist, and each seizing his long scalping knife, and bracing himself, held it high over his head, so as to strike a blow that would carry it to the hilt at once.

"The question of who should be their victim was settled immediately, for as I stepped forward to face that narrow passage of probable death, the chief signaled me back with an impulsive gesture not to be misunderstood, and pointing to Bill, told him to prepare himself for the bloody ordeal.

"I attempted to protest, and was urging my most earnest words, when O-ton-son-e-var said he had decided and 'the young man must run,' adding, that 'even a drop of blood from any one of the knives meant death to both.'

"Each savage stood firm, with his glittering blade reflecting the rays of the evening sun, and on each hard, cold face, a determination to have the heart's blood of their victim.

"The case seemed almost hopeless—it was truly a race for life, and as Bill prepared himself I wished ourselves back on the 'Rock' with only as many good bullets as the number of devils who stood before us, the very impersonation of all the hatred of the detestable red man.

"How well I remember the coolness and confidence of Bill. He could not have been more calm if he had been stripping for a foot race for fun. He had perfect faith in the result, and when O-ton-son-e-var motioned to commence the fearful trial, Bill spoke to me, but I could not answer, my grief was too great.

"He stripped to his drawers, and, standing there, naked from the belt up, was a picture of the noblest manhood I ever saw as he waited for the signal. He tightened his belt, and stood for a few seconds looking, with compressed lips, down the double row of savages, as they stood face to face gloating on their victim. It seemed like an age to me, and when the signal came I was forced by an irresistible power to look upon the terrible scene.

"At the instant, Bill darted like a flash of lightning from the foot of the tree—on rushed the devils with their gleaming blades, yelling and crowding one another, and cutting at poor Bill with all the rage of their revengeful nature. But he evaded all their horrible efforts, now tossing a savage here, and another one there, now almost creeping like a snake at their feet, then like a wild-cat he would jump through the line dashing the knives out of their hands, till at last, with a single spring, he passed almost twenty feet beyond the mark where the chief stood!

"We were saved, and when the disappointed savages were crowding around him, I rushed in and threw myself in his arms. The chief motioned the impatient warriors away, and with sullen footsteps followed them.

"In a few moments we slowly retraced our way to the 'Rock,' where, taking our mules, we pushed on in the direction of the Missouri. We camped on the bank of the Arkansas only a few miles from the terrible 'Rock' that night, but while we were resting around our little fire of buffalo chips, and our animals were quietly nibbling the dried grass at our feet, we could still hear the Kiowas chanting the death song while they buried their lost warriors under the blackened sod of the prairie.'"

A TERRIBLE TEN MILES RIDE.

AN INCIDENT IN THE INDIAN WAR OF 1864.

In all the annals of our "Border Warfare," none will go down to history more conspicuous than the events which crowded the year 1864, on the Great Plains of Kansas, Nebraska and Colorado.

Civilization in those troublesome times still cautiously hugged the extreme eastern belt of our fair young empire, suspicious of the unknown beyond—that immense ocean of grass, stretching interminably toward the setting sun.

The "hunger for the horizon" which to-day marks broad trails even to the very shadow of the mountains, with long lines of white covered wagons, patient oxen, or jaded mules, plodding wearily during the bright hours through the alkali dust of the desert, had not then been stimulated by marvelous stories of fair acres lying so bewitchingly beautiful beyond the "Big Blue."

The magnificent valley of the "Smoky Hill," with its rich share of wooded streams and fertile uplands, or the still more elysian expanse watered by the great Arkansas—that embryo granary of two continents—were simply known as the region through which passed twin inter-oceanic trails—the Oregon and the Santa Fe—both now mere memories.

The Indian summer then as now, wrapped the distant hills in its mellow tints, the grass grew brown and rusty as each recurring season filled its measure, and the autumn days were as grand as Central Kansas ever witnessed, or the golden sunshine ever lighted up. The mirage wove its fantastic forms in the early spring time, and the chain of sandhills that follow the tortuous windings of the Arkansas rested dark and misty—then as now—under the curtain of night. But the Satanic genius of the Indian hatred brooded on the beautiful landscape, and the harvest of the unlabored fields was blood. The empire of the plow had not then dawned, nor the march of the homesteader begun. The "iron trail" was a possibility, but he was a visionist who argued its probability.

From the outskirts of Council Grove, to the crossing of the Cimarron, the echoes of the prairie were awakened by the terrible war-whoop of the savage as he wrenched off the reeking scalp of his hapless victim.

The commerce of the Great Plains over that broad path through the wilderness—the Santa Fe trail—was at its height, and immense trains rolled day after day toward the blue hills which guard the portals of New Mexico. Oxen, mules, and sometimes horses, tugged wearily, week after week, through the monotony of their long journey, their precious freight ever tempting the wily nomads to plunder, dissimulation, and murder. Pawnee Rock, Walnut, Coon, Ash, and Cow creeks, were mute witnesses of a score or more battles that reddened the blossomed prairie in spring time, and the grass of the Pawnee, Heath's Branch and Buckner's, were resonant with the yell of the Kiowas and Cheyennes, who, under the pale moonlight, held their hideous saturnalia of butchery. On the far-off Wolf and Beaver rivers, where to-day, are gathered under the guise of a semi-civilization, the remnants of those once-powerful tribes—the scattered lodges are decorated with the scalp-locks of many who were tempted to brave the perilous duty of freighters, in the year of which we write.

To protect the trains on their weary route through the "desert"—as the whole of this region was then termed, and confidently believed by the world to be—troops were stationed—a mere handful, relatively—at intervals on the "great trail," to escort the freighters, and United States mail over the most exposed and dangerous portions of the route. Many an exciting encounter frequently occurred, and many thrilling incidents, hair-breadth escapes and "moving accidents," belong to the unwritten chapters of the history of those times, the book of which is, in a measure, sealed; for like the ocean, the Great Plains tells but little of its terrible record, and rarely gives up its dead.

The incident which is the subject of this sketch, is as thrilling, perhaps, in its details, and as marvelous in its results, as any that have come down to us in the history of these memorable times.

It deals with plain facts, and of men who are now living —one of whom, the principal actor in the scenes to be related, is known favorably all over the state.

Fort Riley, in the year referred to, was one of the extreme permanent frontier military posts. Here in November, 1864, Capt. Henry Booth was stationed. He was chief of cavalry, and inspecting officer for the district of the Upper Arkansas, the western geographical limit of which extended to the foot of the mountains.

Early in the month, in company with Lieut. Hallowell, of the Ninth Wisconsin Battery, he received orders to make a tour of inspection of the several out-posts, which extended as far as Fort Lyon in Colorado.

Salina was occupied by one company of the Seventh Iowa Cavalry, under command of Captain Hammer. Where the old Leavenworth stage route crossed the Smoky Hill, in a beautifully timbered bend of that stream, was a little log and jacal stockade, commanded by Lieutenant Ellsworth, also of the Seventh Iowa Cavalry.

To this comparatively insignificant post—insignificant only in its appointments, not importance—the commanding officer gave his own name, which the county of Ellsworth will perpetuate in history.

At the crossing of the Walnut, on the broad trail to the mountains, were stationed three hundred unassigned recruits of the Third Wisconsin Cavalry, under the command of Captain Conkey. This was one of the most important points of observation on the "Great Overland Route," for near it, passed the favorite highway of the Indians on their yearly migrations north and south, in the wake of the strange elliptical march of the buffalo to far beyond the Platte, and back to the sunny knolls of the Canadian.

This primitive cantonment grew rapidly in its strategical aspect, was later made quite formidable defensively, and named Fort Zarah in memory of the youngest son of Major-General Curtis, killed by guerrillas somewhere south of Fort Scott, while escorting General James G. Blunt, of Kansas fame.

At Fort Larned, always a prominent place in the military history of the Plains, one Company of the Twelfth Kansas, and a section of the Ninth Wisconsin Battery, commanded by Lieutenant Potter, were stationed. From these troops—the isolated disposition of which I have hurriedly related—squads, consisting usually of from a dozen to twenty men or more, as the case might be, under the charge of a corporal or sergeant, were detailed to escort the mail coach, freighters, government trains, etc.

In the story of these little detachments of brave men, if it could be gleaned in all its thrilling completeness, the escutcheon of Kansas would be made to shine with a more glorious radiance than even now; but, like the purple mist that sometimes creeps over her beautiful valleys, vailing the splendor of the landscape on the other side, tradition is fast relegating the deeds of her early sons to oblivion, and we are

FORT ZARAH.

only permitted at times, in some sweet vision of memory, to catch glimpses of their heroic acts.

On the morning the order to make the special inspection of the out-posts referred to was received at Fort Riley, Captains Booth and Hallowell immediately commenced active preparations for their extended and hazardous drive across the Plains. Rifles and pistols, that had for weeks been idly hanging on pegs against the barrack walls, were taken down, carefully examined and brushed up for possible service in the dreary Arkansas Bottom, and camp kettles were soon busily sputtering over crackling log fires, for the long ride beyond the settlements demanded cooked rations for many a weary day.

All these preliminaries arranged, the question of the means of transportation for the two officers was determined in this wise, and, as the sequel will show curiously enough, saved the lives of the two heroes in the terrible gauntlet they were destined to run.

Captain Hallowell was a famous whip, and prided himself upon his exceptionally fine turn-out which he daily drove around the picturesque hills of Fort Riley.

"Booth," said he that morning, "let's not take a great lumbering ambulance on this trip. If you will get a good team of mules from the Quartermaster, I will furnish my light wagon and we will do our own driving."

"All right," replied Booth, "I'll get the mules."

Captain Hallowell, therefore, had a set of bows fitted to

his light rig, over which was thrown an army wagon-sheet, drawn up behind with a cord, similar to the fashion of the average emigrant outfit now daily to be seen upon the roads of our western prairie. A round hole was thus left at the end, which served as a window, and, as will be seen further on, played a most important part in the tragedy in which this simply-covered wagon figured so conspicuously.

Two valises, containing their dress uniforms, a box of crackers and cheese, meat and sardines, and a bottle of anti-snake-bite, made up the precious freight for the long journey, and in the clear cold of the early morning they rolled out of the gates of the Fort, escorted by Company "L," of the Eleventh Kansas, commanded by Lieutenant Jacob Van Antwerp.

Junction City in those days was in reality the limit of civilization, although Abilene, with its solitary log cabin, and Salina, with only two, made great pretentions as the most westerly cities of the Plains. A single glance at the "howling wilderness" surrounding either place, however, dissipated all idea of possible or probable future metropolitan greatness; still one was regaled right royally even then, so far as the cuisine of Tim Hersey, in his primitive hut on the bank of the Muddy, was concerned, for I doubt if ever prairie chicken, buffalo steak, or antelope has been more deliciously served in the pretentious hotel of 1879, at that place, where now the thousands who annually travel mountain-ward dine with service of silver and cut glass, and wipe their fingers upon damask napkins.

In the morning our little command reached where now Salina nestles so beautifully amidst her heavily fringed streams; the long stretch of magnificent bottom land immediately west of that town was covered with buffaloes, and where the succulent blue stem, keeping pace with our wonderful march of civilization, bows rythmically to the summer breeze, a thick mat of short primitive herbage made that whole region a favorite pasturage for those huge animals, so rapidly passing away to-day.

The rough bluffs that border Alum and Clear Creeks, in Ellsworth county, through which the trail wound its tortuous way, were always, in those days, a favorite haunt of the Indians, and many a solitary straggler has met his death from their swift arrows in what are now called the "Harker Hills."

Safely through these dangerous bluffs and across the beautiful bottoms, that are to-day dotted with some of the most picturesque homes in Ellsworth county, marched the little army, and its one white covered ambulance.

Not an incident disturbed the quiet of the grand autumn day, except the occasional slaughter of a buffalo in mere wantonness now and then by some straggling soldier, and early in the afternoon the stockade in the bend of the Smoky Hill was reached.

After an inspection of this remote little garrison, which was found in excellent spirits and condition, the line of march was resumed next morning for Captain Conkey's camp on the Walnut.

The company of one hundred men, acting as an escort, was too formidable a number to invite the cupidity of the Indians, and not a sign of one was seen as the dangerous flats of Plum Creek and the rolling country beyond were successively passed, and the cantonment on the Walnut was reached with nothing to disturb the monotony of the march.

Captain Conkey's command at this important outpost were living in a rude but comfortable sort of a way in the simplest of dug-outs constructed along the bank of the stream, and the officers, a little more in accordance with military dignity, in tents a few rods in rear of the line of huts.

A stockade stable had been built, with a capacity of two hundred and fifty horses, and sufficient hay had been put up by the men to carry the animals through the winter.

The Captain was a brusque but kind hearted man, and with him were stationed his other officers, one of whom was a son of Admiral Goldsborough, of naval fame. The next morning Captain Booth made a rigid inspection of the place, which took all day, as an immense amount of property had accumulated for condemnation, and when evening came the papers, books, etc., were still untouched, and this branch of the inspection was postponed until the morning.

In the evening, while sitting around the camp-fire discussing the war, telling stories, etc., Captain Conkey said to Booth: "Captain, it won't take more than half an hour in the morning to inspect the papers and finish up what you have got to do, why don't you start your escort out early, and then they won't be obliged to trot after the ambulance, or you to poke along with them; you can then move out briskly and make time?"

Acting upon this suggestion, Captain Booth went over the creek to Lieutenant Van Antwerp's camp and told him he need not wait for the ambulance in the morning, but to march at about half-past six or seven o'clock in advance. So at daylight the escort marched out agreeably to instructions, and Booth continued his inspection.

It was found, however, that either Captain Conkey had misjudged the amount of work to be done, or the inspecting officer's ability to do it in a certain time, and nearly three hours elapsed before the task was completed.

At last everything was closed up, much to the satisfaction of Lieutenant Hallowell, who had been chafing under the delay ever since the troops departed. When all was in readiness, and the ambulance drawn up in front of the commanding officer's tent, Lieutenant Hallowell suggested to Booth the propriety of taking a few of the men stationed there with them until they overtook their own escort, which must now be several miles on the trail toward Fort Larned. So upon this Booth mentioned it to Captain Conkey, who said: "Oh! there's no danger; there hasn't an Indian been seen around here for more than ten days."

If they had known as much about Indians then as they

afterward learned, Captain Conkey's response, instead of assuring them, would have made them insist upon an escort, which Booth, in his official capacity, had the power to order; but they were satisfied, and concluded to push on. Jumping into their wagon, Lieutenant Hallowell took the lines, and away they went rattling over the old log bridge that used to span the Walnut, as light of heart as if riding to a dance. It was a clear, cold morning, with a stiff breeze blowing from the northwest; their trail was frozen hard in some places, and was very rough, caused by the travel of heavy trains when it was wet.

Booth sat on the left side with the whip in his hand, occasionally striking the mules, to keep their speed. Hallowell struck up a tune—he was a good singer—and Booth joined in as they rolled along oblivious of danger as though they were in their quarters at Riley.

After they had proceeded some distance Hallowell remarked: "The buffalo are grazing a long distance from the road to-day—a circumstance I think bodes no good"—he had been on the Plains the summer before, and was better acquainted with Indians and their peculiarities than Captain Booth—but the latter replied, he "thought it was because their escort had gone along ahead, and had probably frightened them away." The next mile or two was passed, and still they saw no buffalo between the trail and the river, but nothing more was said relating to this suspicious circumstance, and they rolled rapidly on.

When about five or six miles from Zarah, on glancing toward the river, to the left and front, Booth saw something that looked strangely like a drove of turkeys; he watched them intently for a few moments, when they rose up and he discovered they were horsemen. He grasped Hallowell's left arm, and directed his attention to them, said. "What's that?" Hallowell cast a hasty look to the point indicated and replying "Indians! by George!" immediately turned the mules and started them back toward Fort Zarah on a full gallop.

"Hold on," said Booth, "maybe its part of our escort?"

"No, no," replied Hallowell, "I know it's Indians."

"Well," replied Booth, "I'm going to see," so stepping out on the foot board, and holding on to the front bow he looked back over the top of the wagon. There was no doubt now that they were Indians—they had fully emerged from the ravines in which they had hidden, and while he was looking were slipping their buffalo robes from their shoulders, taking arrows out of their quivers, drawing up their spears and making ready generally for a red hot time.

While Booth was intently watching their hostile movements Hallowell asked, "they are Indians, a'int they?"

"Yes," replied Booth, 'and they are coming like blazes."

"Oh, my!" said Hallowell, in a despairing tone, "I shall never see poor Lizzie again"—he had only been married a few weeks, and his young wife's name was Lizzie.

"Never mind Lizzie," said Booth, 'let's get out of here;" although he was as badly frightened as Hallowell, but had no bride at Riley, and as he tells it, "was selfishly thinking of himself and escape."

Promptly in response to Booth's remark came back from Hallowell, in a voice as firm, clear and determined as ever issued from mortal throat:

"All right, you do the shooting and I'll do the driving," and suiting the action to the word, he snatched the whip out of Booth's hand, slipped from the seat to the front of the wagon and commenced lashing the mules.

Booth then crawled back, pulled one of his revolvers—he had two, Hallowell only one—then crept, or rather fell over the "lazy-back" of the seat and reached the hole made by the puckering of the sheet, and counted the Indians;—thirty-four feather-bedecked, paint-bedaubed, and vicious a looking outfit as ever scalped a white man, were coming down on them like a hawk upon a chicken.

Booth had hardly reached his place at the back of the wagon before Hallowell—between his yells to the mules—cries out, "how far are they off now Cap."—for he could see nothing in the rear as he sat.

Booth answered him as well as he could, and Hallowell renewed his lashing and yelling.

Noiselessly the Indians gained, for they had not uttered a whoop as yet.

Again Hallowell asked: "How far are they off now Cap?" and again Booth gave him an idea of the distance between

ATTACK OF THE INDIANS UPON CAPTS. BOOTH AND HALLOWELL.

them and their merciless foe, from which Hallowell gathered inspiration for fresh yells and still more vigorous blows.

Booth was sitting on a box containing crackers, sardines, etc., watching the approach of the cut-throats, and saw with fear and trembling the ease with which they gained upon the little wagon; he realized then that safety did not lie in flight, and that something besides mule's heels would be necessary to preserve his scalp-locks.

Once more Hallowell inquired the distance between the pursuing and pursued, but before Booth could answer, two shots were fired from rifles by the Indians accompanied by a yell that was enough to make the blood curdle in one's veins, and no reply was needed to acquaint the valorous driver that the fiends were sufficiently near to commence making trouble. He yelled at the mules, and down came the whip upon the poor animal's backs—Booth yelled, for what reason he did not know, unless to keep company with Hallowell—while the wagon flew over the rough road like a patent baby-jumper.

The bullets from the two rifles passed through the wagon cover immediately between the officers, but did no damage, and almost instantly the Indians charged down upon them, dividing into two parties, one going on each side, delivering a volley of arrows into the wagon as they rode by.

Just as they darted past the mules, Hallowell cried out: "Cap., I'm hit," and turning round to look at him, Booth saw an arrow sticking in his head above his right ear; his arm was still plying the whip, which was going as unceasingly as the sails of a windmill, and his yelling only stopped long enough to answer "not much," in response to Booth's "does it hurt," as he grabbed the arrow and pulled it out of his head.

The Indians by this time had passed on, and then circling back, prepared for another charge.

Booth had already fired at them three or four times, but owing to the distance, the jumping of the wagon and the "unsteadiness of his nerves"—as he declares—the shots had not decreased to any material extent, the number of their assailants.

Down came the red devils again! dividing as before, and delivering another lot of arrows. Hallowell stopped yelling long enough to cry out, "I'm hit again Cap."

Looking around Booth saw an arrow sticking in Hallowell's head, just over his left ear this time, and hanging down his back like an ornament.

He snatched it out, asked Hallowell if it hurt him, but received the same answer as before—"No, not much."

Both were yelling at the top of their voices, the mules were jerking the wagon along at a fearful rate—frightened nearly out of their wits at the sight of the Indians and the shouting and whipping of their drivers. Booth crawling to the back end of the wagon again and looking out, saw the Indians moving across the trail preparing for another charge. One old fellow mounted on a black pony was jogging along in the center of the road behind them, near enough, and evidently intent on sending an arrow through the puckered hole of the wagon-sheet. As Booth looked out, the Indian stopped his pony and let fly! Booth dodged back sideways, the arrow sped on its course and came whizzing through the hole and struck the black-walnut "lazy-back" of the seat, the head sticking way through, the sudden checking causing the feathered end to vibrate rapidly with a vro-o-o-o-ing sound; with a sudden blow Booth struck it, breaking the shaft from the head, leaving the latter imbedded in the wood.

As quick as he could, Booth rushed to the hole and fired at his aged opponent but failed to hit him; while he was trying to get another shot at him, an arrow came flying from the left side and struck him on the inside of the elbow, hitting the nerve or crazy-bone, which so benumbed his hand and arm that he could not hold on to the revolver and it dropped from his hand into the road with one load still in its chamber. Just then the mules gave an extra jump which jerked the wagon nearly from under him, and he fell on the end-gate evenly balanced with his hands sprawling outside attempting to clutch at something to save himself.

At this the Indians gave a terribly yell—of exultation probably, supposing Booth was going to fall out, but he didn't—he caught hold of one of the wagon-bows and pulled himself in again, terribly scared. It was a "close call" and no mistake.

While all this was going on, Hallowell had not been neglected by the incarnate fiends; about a dozen of them had devoted their time and attention to him, but he had not flinched. Just as Booth had regained his equilibrium and drawn his second revolver from its holster, Hallowell yelled, "Right off to the right! Cap., quick!"

Booth tumbled over the back of the seat, clutching at a bow to steady himself, and ' right off to the right" was an Indian just letting fly at Hallowell; the arrow struck the side of the wagon, Booth at the instant fired at the Indian—missed him of course—but he was badly scared, and throwing himself on the opposite side of his pony, scooted off over the prairie.

Back over the seat Booth piled again to guard the rear, where he found a young buck riding close behind and to the right of the wagon, his pony following the trail made by the ox-drivers in walking beside their teams. Putting his arm around one of the wagon-bows, to prevent his being jerked out, Booth quietly stuck his revolver through the hole, but before he could fire, the Indian flopped over on the side of his pony, and all that could be seen of him was his arm around the pony's neck, and from the knee, down one leg. Booth did not fire but waited for him to come up—he could almost hit his pony's head with his hand, so close was he running—he struck at it several times but the Indian kept him close up by whipping him on the opposite side of his neck; presently, the Indian's arm began to work, and Booth looking, saw that he had fixed an arrow in his bow under the pony's shoulder, and was just on the point of shooting at him, with the head of the arrow not three feet from his breast as he leaned out of his hole in the wagon-sheet. Booth struck frantically at the arrow, dodged back into the wagon, up came the Indian, but Booth went out again, for he realized that the Indian had to be got away from there, as he would make trouble. Whenever Booth went out, down went the Indian, up he rose in a moment again, but Booth fearing to risk himself with his head and breast exposed at this game of "hide and go seek" drew back as the Indian went down the third time, and in a second up he came again, but this was once too often. Booth had only gotten partly in and had not dropped his revolver, so as the Indian rose, instinctively, and without taking aim, fired.

The ball struck him in the left nipple—he was naked to the waist—the blood spirted out of the wound almost to the wagon, his bow and arrow and lariat-rope dropped, he fell back on the pony's rump and rolling from there heavily on the ground, with a convulsive straightening of his legs and a characteristic Ugh! lay as quiet as a stone.

"I've killed one of them Hallowell!" yelled out Booth, as the Indian tumbled off his pony.

"Bully for you!" came back the response, and then he continued his shouting and the blows of that tireless whip fell incessantly upon the mules.

All the Indians that were in the rear and saw the young warrior fall, rode up to him, circled around his dead body, uttering the most unearthly yells, but different from anything they had given vent to before.

Hallowell from the cramped position in front, noticed the change in their tone and asked: "What are they doing now, Cap?"

Booth explained to him, and Hallowell's response was more vociferous yelling and harder blows upon the poor galloping mules.

Booth was still sitting upon the cracker-box watching the maneuvers of the Indians, when suddenly, Hallowell sang out: "Right off to the right, Cap., quick!" which startled him, and whirling around instantly, he saw an Indian within three feet of the wagon with his bow and arrow almost ready to shoot; there was no time to get over the seat, and as he could not fire by Hallowell, he cried out: "Hit him with the whip! hit him with the whip!" The Lieutenant suiting the action to the word, simply diverted one of the blows intended for the mules, and struck the Indian fair across the face.

The whip had a knot on the end to keep it from unraveling, and this knot must have hit the Indian in the eye, for he dropped his bow, put his hands up to his face, rubbed his eyes and digging his heel into the left side of his pony, was soon out of reach of a revolver, but nevertheless, he was given a parting shot—a sort of salute—for it was harmless.

A terrific yell from the rear at this moment caused Booth to look around, and Hallowell to inquire: "What's the matter now?" "They are coming down upon us like lightning," replied Booth; and, sure enough, those who had been prancing around their dead comrade were tearing down toward the wagon like a whirlwind, and with a whoop more deafening and hideous than any that had yet preceded it.

Hallowell yelled louder than ever and lashed the mules more furiously still, but the Indians gained upon them as easily as a blooded racer on a common farm plug. Separating as before, and passing on each side of the wagon, the Indians delivered another volley as they charged by.

As this charge was made Booth drew away from the hole in the rear of the wagon-cover and turned his seat toward the Indians, but forgot in the excitement, that in the manner he was sitting—his back pressed against the sheet—his body was plainly outlined probably on the outside.

When the Indians rushed by and delivered their storm of arrows, Hallowell cried out, "I'm hit again, Cap," and Booth in turning around to go to his relief felt something pulling at him; glancing over his left shoulder to learn the cause of the trouble, he discovered an arrow sticking into him and out through the wagon sheet; with a jerk of his body he tore it loose, and going to Hallowell asked: "Where are you hit now?" "In the back," he answered; where looking, Booth saw an arrow sticking, the shaft extending under the "lazyback" of the seat. Taking hold of it, Booth gave it a pull, but Hallowell squirmed so that he desisted. "Pull it out! Pull it out!" he cried. Booth thereupon took hold of it again, and, giving a jerk or two, out it came. He was thoroughly frightened as he saw it leave the Lieutenant's body, for it seemed to have entered at least six inches, and looked as if it must be a dangerous wound; but Hallowell did not cease belaboring the mules, and his yells, accompanying the blows, rang out as clear as before.

After pulling out the arrow, Booth turned again to the opening in the rear of the wagon to see what new tricks the miscreants were up to, when Hallowell yelled again: "Right off to the left Cap., quick!"

Rushing to the front of the wagon as soon as possible, Booth saw an Indian in the act of shooting at the Lieutenant from the left side and about ten feet away. The last revolver was empty, but something had to be done at once, so leveling the weapon at him, Booth yelled "Bang, you son-of-a-gun!"

Down went the Indian, rap, rap, went his knees against the pony's sides, and away he flew over the prairie.

Back over the seat Booth tumbled and began to load his revolver. The cartridges they had in those days were the old-fashioned paper kind, and biting off the end of one he would endeavor to pour the powder into the chamber, but the wagon was tumbling from side to side and jumping up and down as it flew over the rough trail, that more of the powder went into the bottom of the wagon than into the revolver.

Just as he was inserting a ball into the chamber, Hallowell cried out again: "Right off to the left, Cap., quick!" Over the seat Booth went once more and there was another Indian with his bow and arrow in his hand all ready to pinion the

Lieutenant; pointing his revolver at him, Booth yelled as he had at the other, but the Indian had evidently noticed the failure to fire at the first, and concluded that there were no more loads left, so, instead of taking a hasty departure as his comrade had done, he grinned a demoniacal grin and endeavored to fix the arrow into his bow.

Thoroughly frightened now at the aspect things were assuming, Booth rose up in the wagon and grasping hold of a bow with his left hand, seized the revolver by the muzzle and with all the force he could muster hurled it at the impudent brute.

It was a new Remington octagon barrel with sharp corners, and when it was thrown turned in the air striking the Indian muzzle first on the ribs, cutting a long gash.

"Ugh!" grunted the Indian, and dropping his bow and spear, he flung himself over the side of the pony and away he went over the prairie to bother them no more.

Only the one revolver left now and that empty, and the Indians still howling around the apparently doomed men like so many demons.

After he had driven the Indian off, Booth fell over the seat, picked up the empty revolver and attempted to load it, but before he could bite off a cartridge Hallowell yelled, "I'm hit again, Cap."

"Where are you hit now?" asked the gallant Captain.

"In the hand," replied Hallowell.

Looking around, Booth saw that his right arm was plying the whip to the now laggard mules, and sticking through the fleshy part of his thumb was an arrow, which was flopping up and down as his arm rose and fell in its ceaseless and evidently tireless efforts to keep up the speed of the almost exhausted animals.

"Let me pull it out," said Booth.

"No, never mind," replied Hallowell; "Can't stop! Can't stop!" and up and down went his arm, and flip-flap went the arrow with it, until finally it tore through the flesh and fell to the ground.

Along they bowled, the Indians yelling and the occupants of the wagon defiantly answering them, while Booth was still making a desperate but vain effort to load the revolver. In a few moments Hallowell shouted, "they are crowding the mules into the sunflowers!"

Along the sides of the trail huge sunflowers had grown the previous summer and now their dry stalks stood as thick as a cane-brake, and if the wagon once got among them the mules could not keep up their gallop and would soon be compelled to stop.

The Indians seemed to realize this fact, and one huge fellow kept riding beside the off mule and throwing his spear at him and then jerking it back with the thong, one end of which was fastened to his wrist, the other to the shaft of the spear. The mule on the side next to the Indian was jumping frantically and pushing the near mule from the road.

Stepping out on the foot-board and holding on to a bow

with one hand, Booth commenced kicking the mule vigorously; Hallowell, meanwhile, was pulling on one line, whipping and yelling, so together they forced the animals back into the trail and away they shot at the top of their speed.

The Indian kept close to the mules, and Booth made several attempts to scare him by pointing his revolver at him, but he "would not scare," so he threw it at him, missed the Indian, but struck the pony just behind the rider's leg, which started the latter off over the prairie, thus removing the immediate peril from that source.

They were now absolutely without firearms—nothing left but their sabers and valises, and the Indians soon learning that there were no more shots to be feared came closer and closer.

In turn the two sabers were thrown at them as they came almost within striking distance, then followed the scabbards after the yelling fiends as they surrounded the wagon; some rode immediately in front of the mules, impeding their progress, with the most infernal noises and attempts to spear them (the Indians had evidently exhausted all their arrows), and the camp on the Walnut still a mile and a half away.

There was nothing left for our luckless travelers to do but whip and kick the mules and yell, all of which they did most lustily, Hallowell sitting as immovable as the Sphinx, except his right arm, which, from the time he had started, had not ceased, and Booth kicking the poor animals and shouting in concert with their importunate foe. Looking casually back over the seat Booth saw twelve or fifteen Indians coming up behind with their spears all unstrung ready for action, and he felt that something must be done, and that right speedily, to divert them, for if these added their number already surrounding the wagon, the chances were they would succeed in forcing the mules from the trail, and the end of the tragedy soon come.

Glancing around the bottom of the wagon, in his despair, for some kind of a weapon with which to resist them, Booth's eye rested upon the valises containing the dress suits, and snatching his, threw it out, while their pursuers were yet some four or five rods behind.

The Indians noticed these new tricks with a yell of apparent satisfaction, and as soon as they reached the valise they all dismounted, and one of them grabbed it by the two handles and attempted to open it; failing in this, another drew a long knife from under his blanket and, ripping up one side, thrust in his hand, and pulling out a sash began winding it around his head (as a negro woman winds a bandana), letting the tassels hang down his back.

While he was thus amusing himself, another had pulled out a dress coat, a third a pair of drawers, still another a shirt, all of which they individually proceeded to put on, meanwhile dancing around and yelling.

Booth reported to Hallowell how the sacrifice of his valise had diverted the Indians, and said: "I'm going to throw out yours."

"All right," he replied, "let her go, all we want is time." So out it went and shared the same fate as the other.

As long as the Indians were busy helping themselves to the wardrobes contained in the two valises, they were not bothering our horses, and as Hallowell had said, "all they wanted was time."

But while the diversion was going on in the rear, the devils in front and on each side were still attempting to force the mules from the road by rushing at them and yelling, and brandishing their spears; none of them had as yet tried to kill them, evidently thinking they could murder the two officers and secure the animals alive—a prize too valuable for an Indian to lose. But as they were now drawing near the creek, on the opposite bank of which the camp was situated, and the chance of escape grew brighter, one miserable cutthroat of the band conceived the idea, apparently, of killing one of the mules, for he charged down on the wagon, rode close to one and discharging his arrow at him, struck him on the front leg severing a small artery, from which the blood spurted by jerks. The mules had no blinds on their bridles, and the one hurt, seeing the blood, it frightened him so that he gave a terrific jump and started off at a break-neck gait, dragging the other mule and the wagon after him, so all the occupants had to do now was to pound and kick the uninjured one to make him keep up.

This fresh spurt of speed had carried them away from the Indians, but Booth and Hallowell knew that the animals could not continue it, and they became convinced that the Indians now meant to kill one or both of the mules in order to stop them.

The lull caused by the mules outstripping the Indians gave our almost despairing heroes time to talk the matter over.

Hallowell said he did not propose to be captured and taken to Medicine Lodge Creek, or some other place, and then butchered or burned at the leisure of the Indians. He said to Booth: "If they kill a mule and so stop us, let's kick, strike, throw clods or anything, and compel them to kill us on the spot." So they agreed, if worse came to the worst, to stand back to back and fight them off.

This may seem overdrawn to many of our readers of to-day, but if they have ever seen the remains of men and women hacked and mutilated as the writer has, and realize as fully as the occupants of the little wagon did that such a fate awaited them in the event of capture, they, too, would have courted death, sudden, certain and immediate, in preference to that other, more remote but just as sure, and far more terrible.

During the discussion of the situation by Booth and Hallowell, the speed of the mules had slackened but little; the arm of the latter still plied that effective lash, and they drew perceptibly nearer the camp, where there were men enough to rescue them if they could only be made aware of their situation, and as they caught the first glimpse of the tents of the officers and dug outs of the men hope sprang up within them, and life hanging, as it were, by a slender cord, seemed more precious than ever. In the hope of arousing and attracting the attention of some of the soldiers they commenced yelling again at the top of their voices; the mules were panting like a hound on the chase; wherever the harness touched them it was as white with lather as the inside of a shaving cup, and they could not keep on their feet much longer.

Would they hold out until the bridge was reached? provided they escaped the spears of the Indians. The whipping and kicking had little effect on them now; they still continued in their gallop, but it was slower and more labored than before, and as the Indians fell back to make fresh charges, the mules also slackened their gait, and it became almost impossible to accelerate their motion.

Hallowell kept his whip going mechanically, and Booth continued his attention to the little near mule with his foot, but the worn out animal began to evince unmistakable signs of breaking down, and longing eyes were cast toward the camp, now so near.

The Indians that had torn open the satchels had not come up, and did not seem inclined to further continue the fight, but there were still a sufficient number of the fiends pursuing to make it interesting, but they could not succeed in spearing the mules, as at each attempt the plucky little animals would jump sideways or forward and evade the impending blow.

One gigantic fellow followed them with a determination and valor worthy of a better cause—the others seeming now to have almost abandoned the idea of capturing either men or animals, but this persistent warrior, in all probability, was related to the "young buck" Booth had killed, and was thirsting for revenge; at any rate, he was loth to give up the chase, and followed the wagon to within a few rods of the bridge, long after the other Indians had fallen back entirely.

The little log bridge was now reached; their pursuers had all retreated, but the valorous Hallowell kept the mules at the same galloping gait. This bridge was constructed of half-round logs, and of course was extremely rough, the wagon bounded up and down enough to shake the teeth out of one's head, as the mules went flying over the rude structure. Booth called out to Hallowell, "No need to drive so fast now, the Indians have all left," but he answered:

"I ain't going to stop until I get across," and down came the whip, on sped the mules, not breaking their gallop until they pulled up in front of Captain Conkey's tent. Booth could not stand the fearful bounding of the wagon as it rolled across the bridge, so he crawled out behind and walked up to the quarters.

The rattling of the wagon on the bridge was the first intimation the command had of its returning. The sentinel on post had been walking his beat on the east side of the long stockade stable to keep out of the cold northwest wind, and had heard nothing of the yelling and talking until they struck the bridge, when he came around the end of the stable, saw the wagon and two or three of the Indians behind, fired his carbine and thus aroused the camp.

The officers came running out of their tents, the men poured out of their dug-outs like a lot of ants, and the little wagon and its occupants were soon surrounded by their friends. Captain Conkey ordered the bugler to sound "boots and saddles," and in less than ten minutes ninety troopers were mounted, and, with the Captain at their head, started after the Indians.

Lieutenant Hallowell reached the line of officer's tents before Booth, and, as the latter came up, was attempting to rise so as to get out, but each effort only resulted in his falling back. It was thought at first his wounds were the cause, and when asked: "What's the matter; can't you get out?" replied, "I don't know. I can't seem to get up only so far." Some one stepped around the other side to assist him, when it was discovered that the skirt of his overcoat had worked outside the wagon-sheet and hung over the edge, and that three or four of the arrows fired by the Indians had struck the side of the wagon, and passing through the flap of his coat had pinned him down. Booth pulled the arrows out and helped him up; he was pretty stiff from sitting in his cramped position so long, and his right arm dropped by his side as if struck with paralysis.

While Hallowell walked into Captain Conkey's tent, assisted by the Adjutant and Quartermaster, some of the soldiers unhitched the poor mules and led them to the corral. In examining the inside of the wagon twenty-two arrows were found lying in the bottom, innumerable holes through the sheet made by the passage of arrows, besides two from bullets, and the outside of the bed was scarred from one end to the other.

Booth stood looking on while Hallowell's wounds were being dressed, when the Adjutant said: "What makes you shrug your shoulders so, Captain?" Booth replied that he "did not know; something causes it to smart." The Adjutant looked and said, "Well, I should think it would smart; here is an arrow-head sticking into it," and he tried to pull it out, but it would not come. Captain Goldsborough then attempted it, but was not more successful than the Adjutant. The Doctor told them to let it alone and he would take care of it after he had finished with Hallowell, which he soon did, and with his lance cut it out. The point of the arrow had struck the thick part of the shoulder-blade and made two complete turns, wrapping around the muscles which had to be cut apart before it could be withdrawn.

Both of the principals in the terrible ride were soon attended to and made as comfortable as possible. Booth was not seriously hurt, Hallowell, however, had received two severe wounds, the arrow that lodged in his back had penetrated almost to his kidneys, and the wound in his thumb was very painful, caused not so much by the simple contact of the arrow as the tearing away of the muscle by the shaft while he was whipping his mules; his right arm, too, was swollen fearfully, and became stiff from the incessant use of it during his drive, and for nearly a month he required help in dressing and undressing. The mules, the veritable saviours of our heroes, were of little account after their memorable trip— they remained stiff and sore from the rough road and their continued forced speed. Booth and Hallowell went out the next morning to take a look at them as they hobbled around the corral, and from the bottom of their hearts wished them "green fields and pastures new."

About half an hour after the little wagon had returned to Captain Conkey's camp, a portion of the escort which had been sent out in advance in the morning, came galloping up and from them was learned the following in relation to their movements:

They had started from camp early, as ordered the night before, and moved out on a good brisk walk toward For Larned. There were plenty of buffalo on the north side of the trail, and they saw no signs of Indians, except the absence of buffalo near the river. They kept looking back, and slackened their gait somewhat after getting out four or five miles, to enable the wagon to catch up, and when they had proceeded about a mile beyond the point where the Indians made their first attack, and the wagon had been turned toward the camp, one of the lieutenants said to the other that they were getting too far ahead of the Captain, and suggested the propriety of halting, but Van Antwerp, who was in command, thought it better to leave a part of the company at that spot to wait; accordingly a corporal and fifteen men were detailed to remain there until the wagon should arrive, and the balance moved on toward the Fort.

The squad that had been detailed remained by the side of the trail for half an hour or so, when, becoming chilled, the corporal took them toward the river into a ravine that sheltered both men and horses from the cold northwest wind. There they remained sometime, when the corporal, becoming anxious, sent one of the men up to the trail to see if the wagon was coming, but he soon returned reporting nothing in sight. Waiting a few moments longer he sent another man out, who, on returning, reported that the wagon was coming and *had an escort.* This last man had seen them a long way off while the Indians were chasing them, and supposed they were an escorting party—which was correct in one sense, but not as he thought and reported.

Remaining in the ravine until the corporal supposed the wagon had arrived nearly opposite, he moved out his squad on the trail, but seeing no wagon, and suspecting something had happened started his party toward the camp on Walnut Creek. They had proceeded but a short distance when one of the men cried out: "Here's an arrow!" Hardly were the words out of his mouth before a second said: "Here's another!" They knew now the reason the wagon had not come up, and the corporal gave the command to gallop, and away they flew toward the camp. As they successively passed by the empty valises and the innumerable arrows on the trail, they fully realized the kind of an escort that had accompanied the little wagon, when the soldier had reported, "they are coming, and *have got an escort.*"

Captain Conkey's command returned about midnight. He had seen but one Indian during the entire ride, and he was on the south side of the river in the sand hills.

The next morning a scouting party of forty men, under command of a sergeant, was started out to scour the country toward Cow Creek, northeast from Captain Conkey's camp on the Walnut.

When this party had proceeded four or five miles toward their objective point, a corporal reqested the sergeant to allow him and another man to go over to the "Upper Walnut Crossing," to see if they could discover any signs of Indians.

The sergeant, to excuse himself afterward, stated that he supposed the men were simply going over the divide, instead of which they went on until they struck the upper trail and followed it down around the bend, almost to the creek.

When fairly around the bend, and while riding carelessly along, up sprang about three hundred Indians, whooping and yelling! The two soldiers, of course, immediately whirled their horses and started down the creek toward the camp, hotly pursued by the howling savages.

The corporal was an excellent horseman, and led out in their flight closely followed by the private, who was better mounted, but not as good a rider. They had gone but a short distance when the corporal heard the man exclaim:

"Don't leave me! Don't leave me!"

Looking around, he saw his comrade had lost ground, his horse was rearing and plunging, making little headway, while his rider was jerking and pulling on the bit (which was a curb of the severest kind), the corporal called to him and said:

"Let him out! — let him out! Don't jerk him so!"

The Indians were gaining on them rapidly, and soon the corporal heard the man cry out again:

"Oh! don't——!"

Turning his head to see what was the matter, a spear-point struck the visor of the corporal's cap which knocked it off. He had his revolver in his right hand, and thrusting this at the Indian who had thrown the spear, and who was now side by side with him, he fired, shooting him through and through.

No use delaying now, he could be of no assistance to his unfortunate comrade, so leaning forward and sinking the spurs into his horse, the corporal went flying down the valley, with the three hundred Indians in his wake, and making the prairie ring with their hideous yells.

The officers in camp, including Captain Booth and Lieutenant Hallowell, were sitting in their tents when the sentinel on post fired his gun, upon which all rushed out to learn the cause of the alarm, for there was no random shooting in those days allowed around camp or garrison. Looking up the valley of the Walnut, they could see the lucky corporal, with his long hair streaming in the wind, his heels rapping his horse's sides, as flecked with foam the noble animal was straining every muscle as he fairly flew over the brown sod of the winter prairie. The Indians were in hot pursuit, but could not gain an inch on the excited trooper as he tore along toward camp.

In a moment a hundred men had snatched their carbines and run up the creek to the rescue, but the Indians, true to their instinct, turned tail before they came within gun-shot.

The corporal slacked up, rode to the officers' tents, and stopping long enough to give his version of the affair, then went to his quarters.

Captain Conkey started a squad up the creek in a few moments accompanied by an ambulance. They were gone but a short time when they returned with the dead body of the unfortunate private. He had been shot with an arrow, the point of which was sticking out through his breast-bone; his scalp had been torn completely off, and the lappels of his coat and the legs of his pantaloons carried away. He was buried the next day. The main detachment that had gone toward "Cow Creek" returned a little after dark without having seen an Indian.

Evidently the savages that had given Booth and Hallowell

such a terrible ride the day before, were a small war party detached from the large body that chased the corporal, and had gone down the Santa Fe trail to pick up any straggler that might be so unfortunate as to be passing at the time—and the "little wagon" happened to contain those "unfortunates."

If Booth and Hallowell had known of the action of their escort, it would have been better for them, perhaps, if they had continued right ahead instead of turning, as they could not have been more than a mile from the ravine where the corporal had taken his men when the Indians first attacked them. Then, again, as the Indians probably knew just where the escort was, they might have fought still more desperately, in consideration of less time to accomplish their work. At any rate, our two heroes escaped with comparatively slight injury, and could not have done better if they had taken the other course, though the agony would not have been so prolonged. After remaining at the camp on the Walnut for a day or two to recruit their shattered nerves, Booth and Hallowell returned to Fort Riley, and the latter did *"see his Lizzie again."*

The occurrence narrated in this sketch is but one in a thousand; hundreds terminated more tragically, as the nameless graves that dot the prairie along the Santa Fe trail will most assuredly prove.

Many are now living in various parts of the State who were prominent actors in the stirring scenes and "hairbreadth escapes" of those perilous days of the "Border."

Some, too, have risen to positions of honor and trust, while many have passed over "the dark river"—too soon to have witnessed the grand Empire that has grown up on the Great Plains, where they, the hardy pioneers of our marvelous civilization, laid down their lives, a sacrifice demanded by the inevitable and rigorous law of progress in the genesis of grand states.

Lieut. Hallowell, whose bravery and heroism has been but imperfectly portrayed in this "o'er true" sketch, after the terrible ride, succumbed to the dreadful scourge that swept over Kansas in 1867. He was a sub-contractor on the Pacific Railroad, then in process of construction, when that fell disease, cholera, entered his camp, in one of the beautiful little valleys tributary to the Smoky Hill, and while administering to the comfort of his fellow laborers, was himself stricken down. There on the primitive prairie his grave was dug, and all that remained of one of the truest and bravest of men was gently laid to rest with the great circle of the heavens for his monument, and the recurring blossoms of spring time for his epitaph.

Captain Conkey, after faithfully serving his country, retired to the peaceful pursuits of civil life, together with the great army of volunteers, and in the tumult of subsequent events, has been lost sight of.

Captain Booth still lives; has served the State in various capacities, and at present holds the responsible position of "Receiver of the Public Moneys" in the U. S. Land Office, at Larned.

THE MASSACRE AT BABB'S RANCH,

AND A KANSAS WOMAN'S REMARKABLE RIDE.

On the Colorado river, near the source of that stream in Western Texas, some twelve years ago, Babb's Ranch—a snug little *jacal* cabin—marked the extreme limit of frontier civilization, the march of which so wonderful in its strides toward the mountains since that date, was then far east of the ninety-eighth meridian, and the prairies of the Lone Star State, and our own beloved Kansas, a wilderness, into whose magic area the footsteps of the hardy pioneer had not yet ventured. Babb loved the solitude of the grand old motionless ocean around him, and was supremely happy in the society of his little family, consisting of wife, three children, and Mrs. L—— (the heroine of this sketch) a relation by marriage, who had recently become widowed, and who now was making her home temporarily with the Babbs.

The cabin was prettily situated near the bank of a small tributary to the Colorado, and was partially surrounded by thick clumps of elders, plum bushes, and other indigenous shrubs. It contained only one room which served as parlor, chamber, kitchen, and dining-room, but notwithstanding the multifarious uses to which it was put, was kept scrupulously clean through the constant exertions of the female portion of its inmates. A rude ceiling of small saplings covered with mesquit grass formed the floor of a sort of garret which was used as a general "stow-away," access to which was by means of a rude ladder that rested against the wall of the room below.

Early in June, 1867, Babb found it necessary to take the trail for one of the little Mexican towns near the foot of the mountains, and was forced to leave the women and children to take care of themselves. This was done with a sense of perfect security, however, for the Indians had apparently entertained friendly relations, and Babb placing—as many a poor frontiersman has before and since—too much confidence in the humanity of the Comanches, left home with a light heart, and a flattering belief that *his* family, at least, were safe from the murderous knife of the savage. Vain hope! In less than a week after Babb's absence on a magnificent morning in that beautiful June, Mrs. Babb espied several horsemen coming over the ridge about a quarter of a mile away, and as they approached saw with sinking heart they were Comanches, bedecked in all the hideousness of their war-paint. Two of her little ones were innocently playing down in the creek bottom a hundred yards or so from the house, and the first impulse of the mother's heart, of course, was the safety of her darlings. So she ran out, called them with all the love of her soul to come to the house for their lives. She intended to get them inside, bar up the door and stand a siege, the *jacal* walls of the building being almost proof against the bullets of the inferior guns in the hands of the Indians of those days. But the children either not hearing her, or recognizing the fact that it was too late, hid in the bushes, and down swept the savages like the wind. In a moment they had found the two little children out of doors, tied them together with their lariats, and leaving them on the ground, rushed into the house, the door of which had not even been closed, and snatching the baby from it's mother's arms who instinctively essayed to save it, dashed its brains out on the floor. Two of the savages, enraged perhaps, at Mrs. Babb's resistance, immediately jerked the unfortunate woman across the table and inhumanly cut her throat from ear to ear, putting an end to her life and grief at once.

Mrs. L——, who had upon the first dash of the Indians toward the house, rushed up the ladder into the garret, seeing the butchery, gave a shriek of horror, upon which the savages dragged her down and—strange as it may seem—did not kill her, but tying her hand and foot, threw her with the two children across their saddles and galloped off to the North.

General Marcy, who gives a description of this woman's fate in one of his Border Reminiscences, says:

"In accordance with their usual practice, they traveled as rapidly as their horses could carry them for several days and nights, only making occasional short halts to graze their animals and get a little sleep themselves, so that the unfortunate captives necessarily suffered indescribable tortures from harsh treatment, fatigue, and want of sleep and food. Yet they were forced by the savages to continue day after day, and night after night for many weary miles toward the "Staked Plain," crossing *en route* the Brazos, Wichita, Red, Canadian, and Arkansas rivers, several of which were at swimming stages.

The warriors guarded their captives very closely until they had gone so great a distance from the settlements that they imagined it impossible for them to make their escape and find their way home, when they relaxed their vigilance slightly, and they were permitted to walk about a little within short limits from the bivouac; but they were given to understand by unmistakable pantomime that death would be the certain penalty of the first attempt to escape. In spite of this Mrs. L——, who possessed a firmness of purpose truly heroic, resolved to seize the first favorable opportunity to get away; and with this resolution in view, she carfully observed the relative speed and powers of endurance of the different horses in the party, and noted the manner in which they were grazed, guarded, and caught. Upon a dark night after a long and fatiguing day's ride, and while the Indians were sleeping soundly, she noiselessly and cautiously crawled away from the bed of her young companions who were also buried in profound slumber, and going to the pasture ground of the horses, selected the best, leaped upon his back *a la garcon*, with only a lariat on his neck, and, without saddle or bridle started off quietly at a slow walk, in the direction of the North Star, believing this course would lead her to the nearest white inhabitants.

As soon as she had gone out of hearing of the camp, without detection, or pursuit, she accelerated the speed of her horse into a trot, then into a gallop, and urged him rapidly forward during the entire night.

At dawn on the following morning she rose at the crest of an eminence overlooking a vast area of bold prairie country, where, for the first time since leaving the Indians she halted, and turning round, tremblingly cast a rapid glance to the rear, expecting to see the savage blood-hounds in eager pursuit upon her track; but, to her great joy and relief not a single indication of a living object could be discerned within the extended scope of her vision.

She breathed more freely now, but still did not feel safe from pursuit; and the total absence of all knowledge of her whereabouts in the midst of the wide expanse of dreary prairie around her, with the uncertainty of ever again looking upon a friendly face, caused her to realize most vividly her own weakness and entire dependence upon the Almighty, and she raised her thoughts to Heaven in fervent supplication.

The majesty and sublimity of the stupendous works of the great Author and Creator of the Universe, when contrasted with the insignificance of the powers and achievements of a vivified atom of earth modeled into human form, are probably under no circumstances more strikingly exhibited and felt than when one becomes bewildered and lost, in the midst of the almost limitless amplitude of our great North American prairies, where not a single foot-mark or other trace of man's presence or action can be discovered, and where the solitary wanderer is startled even at the sound of his own voice.

The sensation of loneliness and despondency results from the appalling consciousness of being really and absolutely lost, with the realization of the fact that but two or three of the innumerable different points of direction embraced within the circle of the horizon will serve to extricate the bewildered victim from the awful doom of death by starvation, and in entire ignorance as to which of these particular directions should be followed, without a single road, trail, tree, bush, or other landmark to guide or direct—the effects upon the imagination of this formidable array of disheartening circumstances can be fully appreciated only by those who have been personally subjected to their influence.

A faint perception of the intensity of the mental torture experienced by these unfortunate victims may, however, be conjectured from the fact that their senses at such junctures become so completely absorbed and overpowered by the cheerless prospect before them that they oftentimes wander about in a state of temporary lunacy, without the power of exercising the slightest volition of the reasoning faculties.

Such instances of mental alienation, as strange as it may

appear, are by no means uncommon, and I have myself seen several persons whose minds for days were greatly deflected from the channels of sanity.*

The inflexible spirit of the heroine of this narrative did not, however, succumb in the least to the imminent perils of the situation in which she found herself, and her purposes were carried out with a determination as resolute and unflinching as those of the Israelites in their protracted pilgrimage through the wilderness, and without the guidance of the pillars of fire and cloud.

The aid of the sun and the broad leaves of the pilot plant by day, with the light of Polaris by night, enabled her to pursue her undeviating course to the north, with as much accuracy as if she had been guided by the magnetic needle.

She continued to urge forward the generous steed she bestrode, who, in obedience to the will of his rider, coursed swiftly on hour after hour, during the greater part of the day, without the least apparent labor or exhaustion.

It was a contest for life and liberty that she had undertaken, a struggle in which she resolved to triumph or perish in the effort; and still the brave hearted woman pushed on, until at length her horse began to show signs of exhaustion, and as the shadows of evening began to appear, he became so jaded that it was difficult to coax or force him into a trot, and the poor woman began to entertain serious apprehension

---

*Witness the woman found by General Custer in 1868, on the stream in Ford county, north of Spearville—named "White Women's Fork," in commemoration of the fact. H. I.

that he might soon give out altogether and leave her on foot.

At this time she was herself so much wearied and in want of sleep that she would have given all she possessed to have been allowed to dismount and rest; but unfortunately for her, those practical quadrupeds of the plains, the wolves, advised by their carniverous instincts that she and her exhausted horse might soon fall an easy sacrifice to their voracious appetites, followed upon her track and came howling in great numbers around her, so that she dared not set her feet upon the ground; and her only alternative was to continue urging the poor beast to struggle forward during the dark and gloomy hours of the long night, until at length she became so exhausted that it was only with the utmost effort of her iron will that she was able to preserve her balance upon the horse.

Meantime the ravenous pack of wolves, becoming more and more emboldened and impatient as the speed of her horse relaxed, approached nearer and nearer until with their eyes flashing fire, they snapped savagely at the head of the terrified animal, while at the same time they kept up their hideous concert like the howlings of ten thousand fiends from the infernal regions.

Every element in her nature was at this fearful juncture taxed to its greatest tension, and impelled her to concentrate the force of all her remaining energies in urging and coaxing forward the wearied horse, until finally, he was barely able to reel and struggle along at a slow walk; and when she was about to give up in despair, expecting every moment that the animal would drop down dead under her, the welcome light of day dawned in the eastern horizon, and imparted a more cheerful and encouraging influence over her, and on looking around, to her great joy there were no wolves in sight. She now for the first time in about thirty-six hours dismounted, and knowing that sleep would soon overpower her, and that the horse, if not secured, might escape, or wander away, and there being no tree or other object to which he could be fastened, she with great presence of mind tied one end of the long lariat to his neck, and with the other end around her waist dropped down on the ground into a deep sleep, while the famished horse cropped the herbage around her. She was unconscious as to the duration of her slumber; but it must have been protracted to have compensated the demands of nature for the exhaustion induced by her prodigious ride. The sleep was sweet, and she dreamed of happiness and home, losing all consciousness of her actual situation until she was startled and aroused by the pattering sound of horses feet beating the earth on every side. Springing to her feet in the greatest possible alarm, she found herself surrounded by a large band of savages, who commenced dancing around, flaunting their war-clubs in frightful proximity to her head, while giving utterance to the most diabolical shouts of exultation.

Her exceedingly weak and debilitated condition at this time, resulting from long abstinence from food and unprecedented mental and physical trials, had wrought upon her nervous system to such an extent that she imagined the moment of her death had arrived, and fainted. The Indians then approached, and after she had recovered, placed her again upon a horse and rode away with her to their camp, which fortunately was not far distant. They then turned their prisoner over to the squaws, who gave her food and put her to bed; but it was several days before she was sufficiently able to walk about the camp. She learned that her last captor belonged to "Lone Wolf's band of Kiowas."

Although these Indians treated her with more kindness than the Comanches had done, yet she did not for an instant entertain the thought that they would voluntarily release her from bondage; neither had she the remotest conception of her present locality, or of the direction or distance to any white settlement, but she had no idea of remaining a slave for life, and resolved to make her escape the first practicable moment that offered.

During the time she remained with these Indians a party of men went away to the north, and were absent six days, bringing with them on their return, some ears of green corn. She knew the prairie tribes never planted a seed of any description, and was, therefore, confident it was not over three days journey distant to a white settlement, which the party had evidently visited. *

---

* This corn the Indians evidently found at the wood camp of Al Boyd on the Dry Walnut north of Larned. Mr. Boyd informs me that in the year referred to quite a volunteer crop of that cereal grew up in his various camps, and that the harvest, such as it was, was gathered, in all probability by the Indians.—H. I.

This was an encouraging intelligence to her, and she waited the time anxiously when she could depart.

Late one night, after all had become hushed throughout the camp, and everything seemed auspicious for the consummation of her purposes, she stole carefully away from her bed, crept softly out to the herd of horses, and, after having caught and subdued one, was in the act of mounting, when a number of dogs rushed out after her, and by their barking created such a disturbance among the Indians that she was forced for the time to forego her designs and crawl hastily back to her lodge. On a subsequent occasion, however, fortune favored her. She secured an excellent horse, and rode away in the direction from which she had observed the Indians returning to camp with the green corn. Under the certain guidance of the sun and stars, she was enabled to pursue a direct bearing; and after three consecutive days of rapid riding, anxiety and fatigue, she arrived upon the border of a large river, flowing directly across her track. The stream was swollen to the tops of its banks; the water coursed like a torrent through its channels, and she feared the horse might not be able to stem the powerful current; but after surmounting the numerous perils and hardships she had already encountered, the dauntless woman was not to be turned aside from her inflexible purpose by this formidable obstacle, and she instantly dashed on into the foaming torrent, and by dint of encouragement and punishment, forced her horse through the stream, and landed safely upon the opposite bank.

After giving her horse a few moments rest, she again set forward, and had ridden but a short distance when, to her inexpressable astonishment and delight, she struck a broad and well beaten wagon-road, the first and only evidence or trace of civilization she had seen since leaving her home in Texas.

Up to this joyful moment the indomitable inflexibility of purpose of our heroine had not faltered for an instant; neither had she suffered the slightest despondency, in view of the terrible array of disheartening circumstances that had continually confrontered her; but when she realized the hopeful prospect before her of a speedy escape from the reach of her barbarous captives, and a reasonable certainty of an early reunion with people of her own sympathizing race, the feminine elements of her nature preponderated, her stoical fortitude yielded to the delightful anticipation; and her joy was intensified and confirmed by seeing a long train of wagons approaching over the distant prairie. The spectacle overwhelmed her with ecstacy, and she wept tears of joy while offering up sincere and heart-felt thanks to the Almighty for delivering her from a bondage more dreadful than death.

She then proceeded on until she met the wagons in charge of Robert Bent, whom she entreated to give her food instantly, as she was in a state bordering upon absolute starvation. He kindly complied with her request, and after the cravings of her appetite had been satisfied, she desired to gratify his curiosity, which had been not a little excited at the unusual exhibition of a beautiful white woman appearing alone in that wild country, riding upon an Indian saddle with no covering upon her head save her long natural hair, which was hanging loosely and disorderly about her shoulders, while her attire was sadly in need of repairs. According he inquired of her where she lived, to which she replied: "In Texas." Mr. Bent gave an incredulous shake of his head at this response, remarking at the same time that he thought she must be mistaken, as Texas happened to be situated some five or six hundred miles distant. She reiterated the assurance of her statement, and described to him briefly the leading incidents attending her capture and mistake; but still he was inclined to doubt, believing she might possible be insane.

He informed her that the river she had just crossed was the Arkansas, and that she was then on the old Santa Fe trail about fifteen miles west of Big Turkey Creek,* where she would find the most remote frontier house. Then, after thanking him for his kindness, she bade him adieu, and started away in a walk toward the settlements, while he continued his journey in the opposite direction; but he still followed the exit of the remarkable apparition with his eyes, until she was several hundred yards distant, when he observed her throw one of her feet over the horse's back *a la femme sauvage*, and casting a graceful kiss toward him with her hand, she set off

---

* The point where Bent met Mrs. L——, is on the old trail, nearly on the line between Rice and McPherson counties.—H. I.

on a gallop, and soon disappeared over the crest of the prairie.

On the arrival of Bent at Fort Zara, he called upon the Indian agent and reported the circumstance of meeting Mrs. L——, and by a singular coincidence, it so happened, that the agent was at the very time holding a council with the Chief of the identical band of Indians from whom she had last escaped, and they had just given a full history of the entire affair, which seemed so improbable to the agent that he was not disposed to credit it until he received its confirmation from Bent. He at once dispatched a man to follow the woman and conduct her to Council Grove, where she was kindly received, and remained for some time, hoping through the agents to gain intelligence of the two children she had left with the Comanches, as she had desired to take them back to their father in Texas; but no tidings were gained. Meantime she made the acquaintance of a man at Council Grove whom, it is stated, she married, and for aught that is known, may be there yet. Wherever she is I wish her all possible happiness.

It will be readily seen by reference to the map of the country over which Mrs. L—— passed, that the distance from the place of her capture to the point where she struck the Arkansas river, could not have been short of five hundred miles, and the greatest part of this desert plain she traveled alone, without seeing a single civilized human habitation.

If any other woman, in ancient or modern times, has performed as signal, and equestrian achievement as this, I have yet to learn it.

THE SCOUTS' LAST RIDE.

AN INCIDENT IN THE INDIAN WAR OF 1868-9.

The stranger who to-day in a palace-car surrounded by all the luxuriance of modern American travel, commences his "tour of the prairies" at the Missouri River, enters classic ground the moment he leaves the muddy flood of that stream behind him. He sees a large city at the very portals of the "New West" he has journeyed so far to explore, and all the bustle and energy of the grand civilization he sought refuge from, has followed him even here—more than a thousand miles from his eastern home.

Gradually as he is whirled along the "Iron Trail" the woods lessen, he catches views of beautiful intervales, a bright little stream flashes and foams in the sunlight as the trees open, and soon he emerges on the broad sea of prairie shut in only by the great circle of the heavens.

Dotting this motionless ocean everywhere, like whitened sails, are peaceful little homes—true argosies ventured by the sturdy and hopeful people who have fought their way to that tranquillity which surrounds the beautiful picture.

But it was not always so; and however strange it may seem to our traveler, the rare landscape he looks upon from his polished car window has its tale of blood and dark despair, for little more than a decade ago—during the summer and autumn of 1868, three powerful tribes—the Cheyennes, Kiowas, and Arrapahoes waged a relentless and brutal warfare upon the frontier of Kansas and Nebraska, and then another picture was presented, the story of which has gone down to history side by side, with that other terrible one of Wyoming.

Beautiful valleys, and limpid streams, whose margins were fringed with a dense growth of timber, under the shadows of which the clear water rippled along rythmically toward the "Great River;" fields rich in their golden cereals, and primitive homes peeping picturesquely out of the dark foliage of their surroundings, marked the fair region, whose peaceful inhabitants were inhumanly butchered during the raids of these Indians in their devastation of the whole line of settlements from the Republican to the Arkansas.

Men, women, and children were slaughtered with a pitilessness possible only to Indians, their simple little dwellings consigned to the torch, and young girls alone saved from the keen edge of the scalping knife for the horrors of a captivity infinitely greater than death.

The dark sky was illuminated night after night by the glare of burning ranches, and the red glow on the horizon, as the flames died out, carried the terrible tidings to the pallid watchers along the border, that the savages were circling nearer to them in their fiendish travels.

Often young mothers had only time to snatch their little ones from the cradle and dragging an older child by the hand, hurriedly hide in the thick brush on the creek bottoms, while the husband jumping on his horse, alarmed the neighbors, who returning with him, sometimes were successful in driving off the savages.

But this was of rare occurrence, for families so widely separated as they were in that new country could afford but little mutual protection, their houses being frequently twenty miles apart, and before the news could spread or the people gather in some strong log cabin for defense, the Indians came down upon them like the north wind, murdering and destroying whole settlements in a single summer afternoon.

That lovely belt of country between the two rivers was consequently abandoned, and the few settlers who escaped the fury of the Indians were driven into the military posts of Harker and Riley, houseless, homeless and starving. There they were kindly sheltered, clothed and fed by the Government until it was safe for them to return to their abandoned claims and commence the settlement of the country over.

They then found nothing, of course, but the bare land. A little mound of ashes alone indicated the spot where their homes had stood; their fences and cattle were all gone, sometimes wife and children, too—tortured and then murdered or miserable slaves in the hands of the Indians.

But with a determination to surmount obstacles that any other than our noble army of pioneers would shrink from, they took up the axe again and cut their way to the peace and thrift that has gradually increased to what it is to-day in that region.

The condition of affairs on that verge of civilization in Kansas during the years referred to, was much more terrible than the mere outline above attempted. The horrible truths and outrageous brutalities inflicted can never appear in print to shock the sensibilities of a refined people, and the very impossibility of this fact has done much toward creating a false sympathy for the Indians, who, if their diabolical acts were known universally, as they are known to the comparative few, would be declared beyond the pale of the slightest mercy or leniency in the swift punishment that would be sure to follow.

In the middle of September 1868, General Sheridan assumed immediate command of the Department of the Missouri, which included in its geographical area the whole prairie region west of the Missouri river and a portion of the mountains. The famous Seventh Cavalry under General Custer was scattered along the Smoky Hill at Hays, Harker and Wallace, and the Fifth and Third Infantry at the various military posts in the Arkansas Valley and at Fort Leavenworth.

These were the only available troops in this section at the disposal of the commanding General when he determined to organize a winter campaign against the hostile tribes.

The idea of a successful campaign against the Indians of the Great Plains in mid-winter was something entirely novel in border warfare, and had its origin in the wonderful perception and power to overcome military difficulties inherent in General Sheridan.

Heretofore it had been considered beyond the limit of possibilities to make a vigorous war upon the tribes in that season on account of the numberless apparently insuperable obstacles that constantly interpose themselves—the fickle changes in climate—scarcity of grass in some localities for the animals, the obstruction of partly frozen streams, and a thousand and one counteracting influences constantly at work in the desolateness of these remote plains.

The undertaking was regarded by many old officers who had been stationed on the frontier for years as purely visionary, and by plainsmen generally, as experimental at least, with the probabilities of success strongly on the side of the negative.

In almost every instance where expeditions had been sent against the Indians in the spring and summer—the very season which they themselves select for the operation of their implacable hatred of the whites—the result had almost invariably been disastrous to the army, or the effect upon the Indian unsubstantial.

General Sheridan (purposing to profit by the example of General Hancock, his immediate predecessor in the command of the Department, whose expensive and gorgeous campaign of the summer before—gorgeous in its pomp and circumstance—had been futile of results) perceived at once that a termination of the warfare raging along the border every recurring season could effectually be reached only by a severe and decisive blow to the savages in their winter quarters.

To that end, therefore, immediately after the massacre on Spillman Creek early in September, he removed his headquarters from Fort Leavenworth to Fort Harker, on the Smoky Hill, and from thence to Fort Hays, temporarily, until the expedition was organized, which he then commanded in person.

The country knows how completely he succeeded in removing the hostile tribes to their allotted reservations, and how effectually he prevented any further trouble with the Indians in this portion of Kansas, bringing a peace to the region under discussion that will never again be broken by their sanguinary incursions.

Previous to the organization of the winter expedition— about the first of September—General Alfred Sully, who commanded the Military District of the Upper Arkansas, with eight companies of the Seventh Cavalry, and five companies of Infantry, left Fort Dodge on a hurried excursion against the Kiowas, Arrapahoes and Cheyennes, who had been committing depredations in small parties along the border during the summer.

The command marched in a general southeasterly direction from the Arkansas, and reached the "sand hills" of the Beaver and Wolf, by a circuitous route on the fifth day.

When nearly through that comparatively barren region,

they were attacked by about eight hundred of the allied tribes under the lead of the famous Kiowa chief Satanta.

A running fight was kept up with the savages, on the first day in which two of the cavalrymen were killed and one wounded.

The Indians gradually increased their force by new gatherings until they mustered over two thousand warriors—and the expedition was forced to retreat toward the Arkansas.

For four days and nights the Indians hovered around the command, and by the time it had reached the mouth of Mulberry Creek—twelve miles from Ft. Dodge—there are not one thousand rounds of ammunition left.

The incessant charges of the now infuriated savages compelled the troops to use this small amount held in reserve, and they found themselves almost at the mercy of the enemy when they reached the river.

But before they were absolutely defenseless, Col. M. W. Keogh, of the seventh cavalry (afterward killed at the "Rose Bud" in Custer's chivalrous but disastrous battle with Sitting Bull), had sent a trusty messenger in the night to Ft. Dodge for a supply of cartridges to meet them at the creek, which fortunately reached there in time to save that point from being a literal "Last Ditch."

The Indians in that little but exciting encounter, would ride up boldly toward the squadrons of cavalry, discharge the shots from their revolvers, and then in their rage throw them at the skirmishers on the flankers of the supply train, while the latter, nearly all of whom were out of ammunition, were compelled to sit quietly in their saddles, idle spectators of the extraordinary scene.

Many of the Indians were killed on their ponies, however, by those who were fortunate enough to have a few rounds left, but none were captured, as the Indians had taken their usual precaution to tie themselves to their animals, and as soon as dead were dragged away by them.

This essay of General Sully, to feel as it were the disposition of the Indians, determined the question of a sweeping war, and General Sheridan, as we have stated, inaugurated immediate measures to make it decisive and effectual.

Removing his headquarters to Ft. Hays, on the Smoky Hill route, the organization of the winter expedition was immediately commenced.

All the available troops in the department previously referred to, together with the fifth cavalry, which had been ordered to report to General Sheridan for this special duty; picked warriors from among the friendly Osages and Pawnees, and the services of celebrated frontiersmen were called into service.

Desperate duties were required of the famous frontiersmen employed, who, under the general term of "scouts," were expected to carry dispatches, hang on the trail of the Indians, and in the capacity of couriers, keep open communication between Ft. Dodge and the troops operating in that memorable campaign of 1868-9.

These "scouts" were invariably picked men. They were selected with the greatest of care, with special reference to their knowledge of the Indian character and perfect familiarity with the localities of the prosposed field of action, and in the latter capacity guided the troops through the unbroken wilderness of the Central Plains.

Many of these men had passed eventful lives from boyhood among the Kiowas, Arrapahoes and Cheyennes. Some had married and been adopted by these tribes, and not only understood their language perfectly, but had mastered all the original astuteness and strategy of the Indians themselves.

Nearly all of them were identified with the early struggles of the borders, and they rightfully belong to that roll of heroes in the unwritten record of those troublous times in Kansas' history, which has never yet graced the fair pages of our popular magazines, but who may one of these days figure conspicuously in the annals of the country, when all the facts in its memoirs are collected by another and unprejudiced generation.

But they have another history too, which belongs to the tribes among whom they lived so long, that will never die while the Indian remains, though its narration is given only in rude legendary form, to the dusky listeners wrapped in their buffalo robes sitting around the magic circle of the "medicine lodge."

Some of these men still live, and some are quietly rest

ing under the silvery cottonwoods and willows of the far off plains.

The march of civilization over the territory in which their remarkable lives were passed is rapidly obliterating all trace of their simple sepulchres, and absorbing their memory in the uncertain light of mere tradition.

The duties demanded of the "scouts" during the campaign were fraught with danger, desperate venture, and terrible chances for life oftentimes, yet they received no greater reward than was given to other civilians employed.

How nobly these brave men fulfilled their mission, the fight of Gen. Geo. A. Forsyth on the Arrickaree Fork of the Republican (one of the most desperate chapters in Indian warfare, taken altogether, in the history of the continent), General Custer's battle of the Washita, and the grassy mounds in the little graveyard at Ft. Dodge on the treeless banks of the Arkansas where those lie who went out fearessly to their death—all testify.

How two of these "scouts" laid down their lives in a ride of a hundred miles through a gauntlet of determined savages, is the subject of this sketch.

To those who look upon everything in this world with only a utilitarian faith, and measure all operations of human circumstances by the scale of dollars and cents, it undoubtedly seems strange that a remuneration was not demanded and given to these men, corresponding with the awful risks incurred. But there is an indescribable and unconquerable infatuation attending a life in the desolateness of the remote plains, and a companionship of constant danger which lends a charm that can never be perfectly understood by the denizens of our crowded cities in the East, that far out-weighs any tangible reward that could be offered.

Neither the love of gold then, nor the hope of popularity —those two altars upon which so many men sacrifice themselves in the teeming haunts of business—tempted them to the deeds which have made them famous. Such men whose story is always full of interest, seek danger for the simple charm of it, and that alone is the secret of their eventful lives.

Five hundred six-mule army wagons, with its complement of more than as many teamsters, wagon-masters, cooks and herders, composed the transportation train that constantly traveled between the depot at Fort Dodge on the Arkansas, and the base of operations at the camp on Beaver river, (now known as Camp Supply,) and one of the principal posts of observation in the Indian Territory, where the Kiowa and Cheyenne reservations are located.

Over the broad trail marked by the passage of the long train of wagons, the Indians hovered in small parties all winter, and through this line of watchful savages, the courier scout's perilous journey had to be effected.

On their dreary route of over one hundred miles, with no place of refuge between the camp and Fort Dodge, it was literally, at times, a ride for life.

Two of these "scouts" usually traveled together under considerations of both companionship and safety, for it is possible that two determined men well acquainted with the peculiar tactics of the Indians, may prove a match for twenty, but difficult under equal circumstances for one to get away from five.

The most exposed portions of the trail were ridden over at night, while in the daytime, the "scouts" secreted themselves in some rocky cañon or timbered ravine until darkness again favored their lonely trip. Only when within a few miles of their destination at either end of the route, were the chances of a run by sunlight taken.

The characteristic recklessness of some, however, in even essaying this performance resulted in a severe fight on more than one occasion, and the death of two, as the sequel will show, on another.

Two days of hard riding, or rather nights, and untiring watchfulness, were required, to effect the hazardous journey, and none others but the "scouts" attempted it; as when it became necessary for parties connected with the military expeditions to go to either of the posts, they did so under escort of the wagon train, never with the "scouts."

Early in the month of November, two scouts—one a half-breed known all over the plains as McDonald, and the other a white man named Davis, were sent out from Camp Supply by General Sheridan, (who had taken up his headquarters at that point,) shortly after dark with important dispatches for the Government, and a small mail for Fort Dodge.

McDonald was a half Cheyenne, his father had in all probability been a Scotch trapper in the employ of the Northwest Fur Company, thirty or forty years, before but McDonald remembered nothing of him, and had lived all his life with the tribe whose blood flowed through his veins. He was, therefore, an Indian by education, and possessed nearly all their characteristics, with the remarkable exception of a decided friendship for the white race, whose cause he heroically espoused at the commencement of hostilities.

He rarely wore any other dress than the traditional buckskin suit, heavily porcupined and beaded, with its long fringe drooping gracefully from the seams, and on certain occasions adhered most religiously to the tribal fascinations of the war paint, which he then used in the most extravagant manner.

That he was the representative of one of the noblest attributes of human nature, however—faithfulness, which rather than break, he accepted death—will be conceded further on.

Davis was born in Ohio, and had wandered to the Great Plains when he was only fourteen, having been attracted by its mysteries and charms, in 1843, shortly after the appearance of General Frémont's fascinating report of his memorable expedition to the "Rocky Mountains and beyond."

For twenty years he had roamed over the "Far West" making his home near the head-waters of the Missouri and among the Sioux, whose beautiful language he understood perfectly. He had been south of the Platte only a few seasons previous to the breaking out of the hostiles, where he had taken up with a Cheyenne squaw, and was trading with that nation when the war commenced.

The only remarkable characteristic possessed by Davis was a wonderfully quick perception and determination, unexcelled by any other man I ever knew.

All men whose lives have been spent on the plains or in the mountains from boyhood, I am aware, have this element of character in a marked degree usually, which places them in moments of great difficulty and peril far ahead of the Indian, but Davis was strongly superior in this particular; he subordinated it sometimes, however, to an extensive recklessness, which eventually cost him his life.

The days dragged slowly along, and more than a week past without the return of McDonald and Davis to Camp Supply—nothing had been heard of them since they had ridden out in the dark of that cold winter night. Other scouts had come and gone again, but they brought no news of their arrival at Fort Dodge, and of course it was conceded that they were dead—killed by the Indians—but how, or where, was all wrapped in mystery. The wagon train which constantly traveled on the trail from the Camp to the Arkansas brought no information in regard to their fate, and it was believed that like the ocean which never gives up its dead, the great plains had added another silent chapter to its horrors.

Nearly three weeks after the disappearance of the scouts, as the train one afternoon was approaching the low reaches of the Cimarron bottoms, a large party of Indians were observed on the sand hills about a mile and a half away on the opposite side of that river, apparently watching the command. The cavalry were immediately sent in pursuit, which movement as quickly as the Indian discovered they started over the divide and were out of sight in a moment. A squadron of the mounted detachment kept on however, to the spot where the Indians were first seen, but it was not considered prudent by the commanding officer to chase them further and leave the train without all its escort, as this move of the Indians who could no longer be seen, might only be a *ruse* to draw a portion of the troops away, while another war party, possibly secreted somewhere in the interminable sand hills, could dash in, stampede the mules and cut off a portion of the wagons, that locality being peculiarly fitted for such strategy.

Soon after reaching the high sand-knoll from which the Indians had been watching the movements of the train, the troops dismounted and there discovered the first link in the chain of mystery that surrounded the fate of McDonald and Davis.

In a little ravine a short distance from where the horses stood, under a clump of plum bushes, three roughly made graves were found, which the men tore open and resurrected the bodies of three Arrapahoe warriors, wrapped in heavily porcupined and otherwise richly ornamented buffalo robes. The war paint was still fresh on their faces, and their rawhide shields were lying on their breasts. Bows, arrows, and a red-stone pipe were found lying at the side of each, and around the neck of one a circlet of wolf teeth, interspersed at regular distances with the rattles of the rattle-snake—a characteristic ornament.

Through the bodies of two of the dead savages were bullet holes, corresponding in caliber to the Spencer carbine, and another through the neck of the remaining warrior plainly indicated how they had found their death; but by whose hand, and where, and why were they left among the barren sand-hills?

The trail of a large war party was discovered a few rods off from the mouth of the ravine leading from the north, and the imprint of their moccasins in the soft earth indicated they had rested there. These facts connected with other unmistakable signs to the initiated in plains-lore, clearly connected the death of the Indians buried here with the fate of McDonald and Davis, whose bones it was certain were bleaching somewhere between the Cimarron and Arkansas.

The dead Indians were stripped of their trinkets, hurriedly rolled back in their holes and the cavalry rode slowly back to the river, where they found the men cutting the ice and the train ready to cross.

A new interest was awakened among the command, and every man was untiring in his efforts to find out something more in relation to the missing "scouts."

The whole region within protecting distance of the train

was carefully scoured as they moved along by the cavalry, and even the infantry made tedious detours from the direct line of march in hope of unraveling the fate of the unfortunate scouts, but another day passsd away without any further clue, and the command went into camp on the high land between the Cimarron and Crooked creek full of excitement.

On the afternoon of the second day after leaving the Cimarron, as the train was approaching Mulberry creek, further evidence of the death of the scouts was discovered. The commanding officer was riding with Colonel Keogh in advance of the column, intently watching the actions of the Colonel's two hounds, of rare breed, that always accompanied him, and who were evidently on the trail of some animal, when suddenly an immense pack of gray wolves were driven out of the bush by one of the flankers who had been ordered in that direction by Colonel Keogh, and in a moment the frightened pack were scampering over the prairie with all the dogs of the train in full pursuit.

In a short time, and before the wolves were out of sight, the interest of the two officers in those animals were interrupted by a young lieutenant, who came galloping up to them from the rear of the train, holding in his hands a pair of new pantaloons that had been saturated with blood, but which was now dry.

"Major," said the lieutenant, saluting the commanding officer, "one of my men found this near the creek, and I think it has a story if we can read it, that will tell something more about the fate of McDonald and Davis."

The commanding officer scanned the bloody cloth a moment, and handing it to Col. Keogh for inspection, replied: "Evidently those pantaloons have been torn from the wearer; they were never taken off in the ordinary manner, for you can see they are still buttoned, and I imagine the Indians and Coyotes have had a hand in it; Col. Keogh and myself were just wondering what so many wolves—pointing with his glass to the pack in the distance—were doing here on the creek—there is certainly some unusual cause to attract them, and now their presence confirms your suspicions, and I believe myself we shall find out something here in regard to the missing "scouts" or some one else who has been murdered by the Indians."

Col. Keogh suggested the propriety of camping there, and the Lieutenant stated there was plenty of wood and water.

"You may stop the train," said the Major, addressing himself to the Adjutant who had now joined the little group that had gathered where this conversation took place. "We will go into camp on the creek—it is early yet, and perhaps we can find out all about the matter before dark. As soon as the men get their dinners, order every one who can safely leave, to make a thorough search all over the prairie, and up and down the creek."

The Adjutant rode back, halted the train, and the command, among whom the story of the bloody pants had now circulated, went into camp, cooked their dinners as quickly as possible, in order to get all the daylight they could in which to find out something more of the sad fate of McDonald and Davis.

As soon as dinner was disposed of, the sentries posted and the mules and horses picketed near the wagons, several details were made by the Adjutant to search through the creek bottom, and a detachment of the cavalry ordered to scour the open prairie on all sides, to find out if possible the secret of the bloody pants.

In about half an hour after all the details had left the camp, one of the cavalry soldiers of the searching party returned, rode up to a group of officers who were smoking their pipes around a blazing fire of old logs, near the bank of the creek, and reported that some of the infantry had just found two dead horses and an empty mail sack down in the bottom.

"The letters have all been torn open," said the trooper, "here is one I picked up (handing it to the Adjutant who stood by) signed by Col. Crosby. Three or four of the men say they know the horses, and that they are the same ones that McDonald and Davis rode away from Camp Supply—two bays—they are nearly eaten up by the wolves, but I guess there's enough of their skin left to tell their color."

"In which direction," said the Adjutant, "up or down the stream."

"Up the creek," he replied. "You see that dead Cottonwood," pointing to a tree whose top could be seen above the banks of the stream less than an eighth of a mile away. "Well, right there, there is a little open spot, near the tree, and up the creek, two or three rods from it, are what is left of the horses in the brush—you can't miss it because a good many of the men have gathered around there. Look! you can see some of them now out on the prairie, opposite the place."

The soldier rode back up the creek after imparting this information, and all of the officers who were not on duty ordered their horses and started for the "dead Cottonwood."

In a few moments the place indicated by the soldier was reached, where the commanding officer and Col. Keogh with about twenty men were found.

Lying in a thicket of hazel, close by the water, were the two horses with the flesh partially eaten off their bones, and a small canvas mail bag fastened to an overhanging limb—where it had evidently caught in an attempt to throw it in—was dragging in the stream.

The contents of the mail sack were strewed over the ground in every direction, the letters torn open, and the dispatches from the government a mass of pulp on the edge of the stream. A few cartridge shells were scattered around, and from the tracks in the soft mud of the bottom, it could easily be seen that a stand had been made at this point by the unfortunate men.

The Indians knew, as early as that time, that letters occasionally contained money, and that fact accounted for the demoralized condition of the "scouts'" dispatches. The numerous raids of the savages on the Overland Stage Routes had taught them the value of a mail sack—they evidently thought to profit by their experience in this instance, for these pirates of the prairies, while they are opposed to the encroachments of the white man within their domain, accept with avidity all the conveniences which civilization brings to them.

They had learned the value of our medium of exchange for the power it gives them to secure from the trader those things they covet, at a fairer equivalent than in the uncertain complications of direct barter; so that money now taken from their prisoners is no longer destroyed as worthless, or thrown away, but has assumed a value which is being more perfectly understood every year, without a labored study of political economy.

The scattered mail was carefully collected, put in the original sack and sent back to camp, while the search for further developments in this melancholy episode was continued through the timber on the margin of the creek, and upon the broad prairie on either side, but night came on without anything new being discovered, and early next morning the train went on its way to Fort Dodge.

The search, of course was reluctantly abandoned, as not even the solution of the mystery which now seemed almost within the grasp of those whose interest had been so thoroughly awakened, could subordinate the duty of the train for a single day.

The train reached Fort Dodge early the following afternoon and commenced taking in its immense freight of corn and oats immediately, in order to return as soon as possible to the spot where McDonald and Davis had evidently given up their lives.

A short rest of a few hours for the men, while some repairs were being made to the paraphenalia of the train, was all the delay permitted by the commanding officer, and by noon the long column of wagons rolled out once more with now a double duty for its mission.

The camping place was made at the same spot on Mulberry Creek where it had camped before, and where the "scouts'" horses and the mail were found.

The creek was reached about four o'clock that afternoon —too late for any active work, and the command retired eager for the first glimpse of morning.

As soon as it was fairly daylight, the animals were picketed within the line of sentries, all the usual precautions being taken to prevent a surprise by the Indians, and breakfast disposed of, every effort was made to find the bodies of the missing Scouts, as all felt certain they had been killed in that vicinity, and left where they had fallen, for the Indians have no compunctions in leaving a white man food for the wolves when they have secured his scalp.

Every available man in the whole command—civilian and soldier—was detailed to go carefully over the whole country within a couple of miles of the camp, in parties sufficiently strong to protect themselves from any small number of Indians that might dash down upon them from the hills, while the region within that radius was pretty well picketed and overlooked by the sentries, who were stationed on all the highest points of the bluffs, and could see the enemy no matter what direction they might come from, and give the alarm by firing a gun, which would of course give all those who were out, ample time to prepare for any contemplated attack.

The search was continued all day without results, until just before sun-down, when a party of cavalry that had ventured out at a greater distance than the rest of the command, sent a detachment back to camp with the news that they had found the remains of the scouts, and orders to return with a wagon to bring them in.

The commanding officer, Colonel Keogh, and four or five others, upon the receipt of this intelligence, mounted their horses and rode out to the place indicated by the soldier, who remained to conduct the wagon and the escort of infantry that had been ordered to go with him.

After a brisk gallop of ten or fifteen minutes, the officers reached the company of cavalry who had been dismounted and were lying on the ground, discussing the terrible fight that must have taken place before McDonald or Davis succumbed, as their pluck and desperate character under such circumstances were well known.

Near where the squadron of cavalry had halted, on the side of a hill sloping toward the creek, were discovered the ghastly skeletons of the unfortunate scouts, bleaching in the cold winter sun. A leg had been dragged here, and an arm there by the half famished wolves, who had devoured every particle of flesh off the bones of the two men. One of the skulls, supposed to have been Davis', was only found after a diligent search, a quarter of a mile away, where it had been carried by a wolf and then dropped.

The other skull, McDonald's, was crushed into atoms, and was found near the remainder of his skeleton.

Davis had been shot through the head at least three times, as that number of bullet holes were plainly discernable, and on the back of it great chips had been hacked out as if done with an axe.

There was nothing to indicate in the surroundings of the place where the remains of the two skeletons were found, that that spot had been their last stand; it was evident they had met their death elsewhere, and had been dragged to where they were lying by the wolves, but as it was too late to investigate further, the matter was abandoned for the present.

Nearly all of the bones of both men were collected, wrapped in a rubber poncho and taken to camp, where they were covered over with a pile of rocks to prevent the wolves from scattering them over the prairie again, and left until the train returned from Camp Supply when they were taken to Fort Dodge and given a christian burial.

The next morning the train went on to its destination, and a few days afterward returned and camped on the old ground to seek for further developments. On the evening of that day the Commanding Officer with Colonel Keogh and two or three others, discovered the exact spot where the brave scouts had met their death in the thick brush more than a mile from where their skeletons had been found. A scarred and blotted tree, from one of the limbs of which was suspended a bloody rope, stood alone in a little opening on the bank of the stream, encompassed by rocky bluffs, from the top of which could be seen Fort Dodge and the silent waters of the Arkansas.

The rough bark of this tree was torn by a hundred bullets, and its gnarled trunk pierced by as many arrows. At its foot was lying a broken spear, and the ground all round was covered with cartridge shells. Dark patches, that had once been little pools of blood, matted the dead grass at its roots, all of which told more expressively than any language the story of the horrid scene that had been enacted there.

A few of these mute witnesses were collected, and the party returned to camp having fulfilled its mission, but the thoughts of the awful and hopeless fight that had broken the silence of that winter prairie settled a feeling of sadness over the whole command.

After the battle of the Washita, and white winged peace brought the tribes in friendly relations with the white man once more, some of the facts in this tragedy were elicited from the very Indians who had taken part in it.

From them was learned the story of the fight in this wise: "A party of Arrapahoes, numbering nearly eighty, discovered the two scouts about sixteen miles from Fort Dodge, early in the afternoon of the second day after they had left Camp Supply. The Indians tried to surround them on the open prairie before they could reach Mulberry Creek but McDonald and Davis were too wary, knowing full well the terrible consequences if they permitted themselves to be taken alive.

"The savages circled around them but did not fire a shot, hoping, as they all the time drew nearer, to surround them before they could reach the creek.

"It was a terrible race for life, and all the cunning and strategy of the Indian and white man was called into requisition, each endeavoring to circumvent the other.

"The scouts rode for the friendly timber on the creek in front of them—but still so far away—with all the confidence of their nature stretched to its utmost, feeling certain that could they but reach it, the Indians would be outwitted by the tactics of the white man.

"But it was destined to be otherwise. Not a shot had been fired yet on either side, and the scouts saw the refuge of the dead and leafless trees almost within reach—they saw also in the hazy distance the flag at Fort Dodge, gleaming and twinkling in the sunlight as they reached the crest of the hill towering above the narrow bottom of Mulberry Creek, when, at a sign from the chief, a young warrior stopped, jumped off his pony and pulled up his rifle just as McDonald, who was a little in advance, entered the low sumac bushes skirting the timber. The Indian fired, killed Davis' horse and the scout found himself on foot, with twelve long miles between where he stood and Fort Dodge.

"The Indians gave a yell of exultation as they saw Davis' horse fall, and in another instant McDonald's horse was shot too, the red devils having purposely avoided hitting the men before, determined to take them alive if possible.

"Here the two scouts stood at bay for a few moments, utilizing the carcasses of their dead animals for a breastwork, from behind which they killed two of the murderous fiends in front of them.

"One of the Indians now rode up to within a hundred yards of where the scouts stood bravely together, and made a sign to McDonald to talk with him. McDonald stepped out a rod or two in advance of the spot where he had stood to listen to the Indian, who said to him:

'Leave Davis and come to us—you are our brother—we do not want to kill you; we will give you your life to get the white man's scalp.'

"But McDonald heroically answered the savage, while he stood in front of Davis, that the white man was his brother too—that he could die with him, but could not leave him; he then pulled the trigger of his rifle, which he had drawn up as he said this, and sent the ball into the very throat of the Indian who had made the proposition.

"This exasperated the remainder of the Indians, who rushed upon the unfortunate scouts, and drove them from their little shelter, up the creek to the lone tree where they laid down their lives. And there they stood shoulder to shoulder until McDonald fell; then Davis fired shot after shot as rapidly as possible, killing two more Indians, one of whom was the chief, (whose grave was found with the others by the train in the sand-hills of the Cimarron)."

The Indians never would tell the meaning of the bloody rope, but that it was an important factor in the orgies which took p'ace over the dead bodies of the scouts no one can doubt.

The broken spear, arrow heads, and some of the cartridge shells the writer has preserved in the East, which will be transferred to the rooms of the Kansas State Historical Society, as has the letter from General Sheridan, (found in the scattered mail on Mulberry Creek as related,) herewith copied:

HEADQUARTERS DEPARTMENT OF THE MISSOURI,
CAMP SUPPLY, November 3rd, 1868.

MY DEAR MAJOR INMAN: I send out two scouts this evening to see how you are getting along with the train. Send them back in advance of you to let me know where you are.

* * * * * * * *

Yours truly, P. H. SHERIDAN,
Major General.

The truth of this tragedy, in all its details, will probably never be known, for the Indians, who were the principal actors, were reticent as is their wont, and only what has been related, in a rude manner, could be gathered from them.

It is the impression of the writer, however, that the unfortunate men were captured and tortured, the evidence all pointing so strongly in that direction—but this the Indians denied. But if they really were killed as stated by the savages, who, even then, in the quiet of his own home, can realize what the scouts suffered, as they stood shoulder to shoulder against that scarred and blasted tree hopelessly defending themselves from the overpowering number of red fiends opposed, with the fort in sight from the top of the bluffs just above them; or how immeasurably less can be imagined the feelings of Davis as he saw his faithful comrade fall—how despairingly he must have clutched his rifle as his stock of cartridges was fast diminishing; how earnestly he must have looked toward the horizon for some hope of help that never came. As the wind was sadly sighing his requiem, he sunk to his death as the last gleam of golden light flooded the hills—so the horrid picture before him ended in eternity.

In the campaign of 1868-9, in which the above related incidents occurred, were many men who are now living in Kansas who took a prominent part in the stormy times of those dreary months, who, if this short sketch should happen to fall under their eyes, will recognize the facts in the death of the scouts as given. Their names would occupy too much space if it even were possible to collect them. Many of them, too, among whom was the brave Colonel Keogh, and other gallant officers and soldiers of the famous Seventh Cavalry—were killed in the disastrous battle of the Rose Bud in Custer's reckless and unsupported charge on the camp of Sitting Bull. Many of those, too, who participated in the arduous work of that winter's campaign have held, and are now filling responsible positions all over the state. Among them are Messrs. C. C. Sprigg, J. F. Dyer, and Geo. Huyck, respectively Clerk, Register of Deeds, and Treasurer of Ellsworth county, and Hon. Paul T. Curlett, Chairman of the Board of Commissioners, Pawnee county. Pat Sherman, on the police force of Topeka, was Chief Wagon-Master of the train that moved all winter between Dodge City and Camp Supply, and Larry Dieger, late Marshal of Dodge City, was his assistant.

"WAL HENDERSON."

In one of the busy little mining camps just over the range in New Mexico, there prowled around about ten years ago, a notorious character, whose life was made up of desperate adventures, and whose tragic death, which is the subject of this sketch, illustrates the inevitable fate of the average border bully.

"Wal Henderson" was born and "raised"—as he termed it—in Missouri, and came over the mountains into the New Mexico mines from Colorado soon after the first discovery of gold in the Moreno hills, where he staked off a claim in Humbug Gulch, and commenced working in an apparently honest way. He was a rough, illiterate fellow, possessing the physique of a giant, courageous as a she grizzly with cubs, and such a dead shot with his revolver, that he soon became a terror to the whole mountain population; in fact he was a desperado in its fullest sense, without one redeeming quality, except that he was kind to his dog, a mangy, spotted, wicked-looking cur, fit companion for such a surly master.

Any more intercourse with Wal, than was absolutely necessary, was carefully avoided by every one, and such an idea as getting into a dispute with him—who would rather shoot than eat—never entered the heads of those who worked claims in the vicinity, so that, virtually, he commanded the respect of a king. One afternoon Wal was seized with a desire to start off on a little prospecting tour to another portion of the range where he suspected the existence of a quartz lead, so he left his claim in the "Gulch" only partially opened, never dreaming for an instant that any one would have the temerity to jump it in his absence, after they discovered he owned it, and which he took good care they could easily learn, for before he went away he asked one of his more educated neighboring miners to "come over and cut his name" on a dead pine stump that stood near the mouth of his pit.

This friend was nothing loth to oblige his surly comrade, so just after dinner he came over, when with his keen bowie knife he slashed out a huge

"WAl henDerSoN his KLAime,"

on the dead stump.

It took him nearly two lours to complete his literary labors, while Wal stood by impatiently watching him, who when his friend had just finished the last touch of his rude letters, remarked:

"Well, I guess there haint no one goin for to touch that thar," and swinging his pick and shovel over his shoulder he whistled to his dog, and then taking his bearings by a look at the sun started down the cañon on a sort of shuffling trot, and was soon out of sight.

He was gone three days and when he returned found

that his ground had been "jumped" by a party of Irish miners who had come into the diggings during his absence.

"Wal in as quiet a manner as his bull-dog nature permitted, told them "to git!" But they swore that they would hold it in spite of him, and if he was as big as "Finn MaCool" they would fight him.

Wal smothered his rage for the moment, cooly walked off to his cabin, and arming himself with two revolvers a Spencer carbine, and a wicked looking IXL blade started back to the gulch, determined to drive the intruders away or kill them if necessary—it mattered little as to choice.

"Git out of this!—quick!—jump! or I'll fill you full o'holes!" was "Wal's" greeting as he came in sight of the intruders on his return; upon which one of the plucky, but unfortunate Irishmen made a break for Wal, to finish him by a well directed blow from his miner's shovel.

Wal quick as thought brought down his revolver and killed his man instantly—the bullet hitting him in the forehead directly between the eyes—a spot that was "Wal's" invariable target, and which in his list of nearly a score of victims, he never had failed to center.

The two now thoroughly frightened companions of the dead miner fled to camp and told the story of the murder.

"Wal" believing that he would have a crowd on his heels in a little while, made his way hurriedly to his cabin, proposing to "lite out" for a while as he said, but a mob of plucky men intercepted him, and he was arrested, taken to camp, confined in a little log building and a guard placed around it.

As the news spread around the hills of "Wal's" latest exploit, the Irish miners came flocking in from all directions, and the people of the town expected a general outbreak between the Irish and American element, if any resistance was offered to the infuriated friends of the murdered man in their attempt to take Wal from the improvised jail, which they openly proclaimed they intended to do as soon as night came on.

The building used for the incarceration of Wal, was an abandoned log store about sixteen feet square; the interstices of the logs were chinked with mud, and the whole surmounted by a brush and dirt roof. In the corner of the room—after the Mexican fashion—a huge, but rude fireplace had been constructed of stone and earth, from which a large chimney composed of the same material communicated with the open air through the roof above.

No sooner had the heavy door closed on Wal than he began an accurate survey of his quarters, with a view of escaping as soon as the mob he confidently expected should make their appearance.

One glance at the immense fire-place, which yawned like the opening to a cave, and a look at the clear sky above through the chimney, satisfied him that he would be out of his prison, and up some mountain gulch before his intended captors could think twice.

Shortly after dark a motley crowd of rough miners, half crazed with the villainous liquors they had been drinking all the afternoon assembled at the jail, and ordered the guard away, fired their pistols in the air, and made the very hills ring with their curses and imprecations upon the prisoner within the little hut.

Wal meanwhile had determined to escape, and in fact at the very time the crowd had reached the door, was on the roof quietly waiting for the mob to make a rush inside, when he proposed to leap to the ground from the rear of the building.

He waited for the signal, which soon came in the shape of a volley of pistol and carbine shots, and a wild yell from the would-be avengers, who with a desperate rush made for the door of the jail, which under the pressure flew from its fastenings and swung open with a loud report, throwing half a dozen of the mob upon the dirt floor.

For a moment or two no one could enter, as those nearest the door became wedged together, while the pressure from the crowd in the rear held them more securely imprisoned than Wal, who at this juncture jumped from the roof, and to use his own expression "lit out d——d lively."

When the crowd became aware that Wal had escaped, they threatened to lynch the guard, and but for the intercession of some of the cooler-headed and less drunken members of the party, no doubt their threats would have been carried into execution.

They divided up into little bands and scoured the camp, visiting every suspected house or hole where their game might possibly be secreted, and it was not until early morning that the search was abandoned.

The following day the events of the preceding night were fully discussed, and as many conjectures were suggested in relation to Wal's escape and present whereabouts, as there were groups of men; each had his own theory, each knew exactly how and when he got away.

Old Sam Bartlett, a short, thick-set, grizzly, veteran miner, who had whacked bulls on the Santa Fe trail, had lived for months on hard tack and bacon in the mountains of California and in Nevada, who had years before fillibustered with Walker in Nicaragua, and who, altogether, had seen about as eventful a life as any man of his age, expressed it as his opinion "that Wal went up that thar chimbly, and by this here time was well heeled somewhar near camp surrounded by a battery of small arms, and ready to fight the whole outfit."

Sam's surmises proved true, as it afterward appeared, for no sooner had Wal made good his escape, than he went to his own den for a moment, to secure arms and ammunition, and then to an abandoned tunnel about a mile up the nearest gulch, where he immediately commenced to fortify his position, and prepared to sell his life as dearly as possible if the mob pursued him, or, as he afterward said: "Did not intend to pass in his checks, until he had made a sieve of a few of 'em."

The Mexican woman with whom he lived proved a faithful ally, and secretly conveyed, under the shadow of the night, food and his blankets, never revealing to a soul where her Americano was, and always earnestly denying any knowledge of the fugitive.

For nearly a week Wal lived in the abandoned mining tunnel, at the expiration of which time, when the excitement had somewhat subsided, and it being generally supposed that he had fled the country, he quietly walked into camp at midnight, broke open a stable, took out a horse, saddled him and galloped off to Taos, which place he reached next morning. In justice to Wal, let it be known he was not a professional horse-thief—he had not gotten so low as that—but having perfect faith in the old saw that "self-preservation is the first law of nature," seized upon the only reliable means to escape strangling by a mob, and on his arrival at Taos, where he felt secure, returned the animal to his owner with thanks, complimenting him on his architectural skill in constructing a stable that could be entered so easily, and upon the endurance of his horse that had carried him so well.

A little more than a month later, the camp was somewhat startled one afternoon at seeing Wal come riding down the main street mounted on a Mexican pony, with four revolvers buckled around his waist, and a carbine slung across his back. Halting in front of Joe Stenson's saloon, he alighted and with a devil-may-care sort of a nod to the loafers hanging around, invited them all in to take a drink. To the crowd at the bar he related his adventures since he had been among them, said he was tired of Taos, and came back to look after his mining interests up Humbug Gulch which he thought he had neglected too long, and added "if any gentleman (?)" were sympathizers with the would be stranglers, he would be pleased to step out on the street and give them an exhibition of his peculiar manner of managing the portable battery he had provided himself with No one seeming particularly anxious of witnessing the proffered entertainment, war was not declared, and after a round or two of Taos lightning, as whisky was called in those days, Wal quietly mounted his horse and made his way toward his little log hut, where he was met by his faithful Senora and provided with a bountiful repast of tortillas and frijoles (corncake and beans).

The excitement in camp gradually exhausted itself, and it was mutually agreed that Wal should not be molested if he kept away from Humbug Gulch.

Wal apparently accepted the situation, and turned his attention to the laudable ambition of supplying the camp with cord-wood, and almost any day thereafter he could be seen coming into town with his load, which brought him a fair price and ready sale.

One day about two months after he had settled himself down to legitimate pursuits, while he was sitting in Stenson's saloon, fatigued by a somewhat arduous morning's work, a party of Irish miners entered, all of whom were more or less under the influence of liquor, and after bandying words with Wal in reference to his claim and the murder of their companion, one, rather more bold than discreet, approached Wal holding a large rock and said: "Be jabers, Wal, you would look better dead than alive," when Wal, as quick as thought, drew his pistol and drawing a bead on the Irishman, said: "Drop that stone."

The stone dropped, Wal quietly resumed his seat without another word, replaced his pistol in its scabbard, cooly lighted his pipe and commenced to smoke. The gang were evidently bent on mischief, but Wal could not be intimidated and made no move to leave his seat, but kept his keen eye on every act of the drunken mob.

He listened cooly and indifferently for a while to their coarse jets and braggadocio threats cast at him, but there comes a moment when "patience ceases to be a virtue" and comes soonest to men of such caliber as Wal, and when another of the belligerents approached too near with an outrageous remark, Wal jumped to his feet and said: "By G—d, I think I'll kill one of you just for luck, and put a stop to this d—d nonsense," and whipping out his pistol fired, the ball as always, taking effect in the bridge of his victim's nose, passing through the right eye and coming out in front of his ear."

At the report of the pistol a crowd rushed in, but no one attempted to interfere with Wal, who took a position against the side of the room and invited any one who wanted him to "step right up, but if anyone did, he would make a sieve of him."

No one desirous of being converted into that useful article just then, not a soul stepped forward.

The Alcalde and Sheriff were sent for and soon arrived, whereupon Wal gave himself up, and was remanded to his old quarters—the little log jail—from which he had so successfully made his escape by way of the huge chimney, on a former occasion.

The drunken companions of the murdered miner immediately upon the arrest of Wal started off to muster up a crowd of their countrymen, determined this time to mete out summary vengeance upon the assassin of their comrade.

To preclude the possibility of an escape on the part of the prisoner, an additional guard was employed to watch the outside of the jail, and two men were posted on the roof—"no goin' up that thar chimbley this time."

Shortly after dark another mob composed of the friends of Wal's last victim came pouring into camp from the gulches and hills, who proceeded directly to the jail, determined this time that their game should not slip through their fingers.

In a few moments the infuriated and howling would-be lynchers forced the door of the building open, in the same manner as they had done before, but their bird had flown—Wal was not there!

Knowing the desperate character of the men who had come to take his life, Wal resolved to make a determined effort to get away from them, if possible, and when he first heard them surging and howling in the distance, put all his quick wits at work and soon decided what might be done.

Standing at the side of the door as it was crushed from its fastenings, he allowed the crowd to tumble and rush pell-mell into the dark room, while he quietly slipped past them out into the street, walked slowly to the first corner, and then shot into the night—and was free.

The rage and disappointment of the exasperated miners' on the discovery that their man had eluded them can better be imagined than described.

Wal proceeded to his little home, took one of his horses from the stable and rode rapidly out of camp and over a mountain trail, and in a few hours was miles away where he found a safe retreat.

The disappointed crowd on discovering that for the present at least, Wal was beyond their power, slowly retired to their homes, but first swore they would kill Wal on sight if he ever made his appearance in camp again.

But a few days elapsed before Wal again dropped into town, but strange as it may seem no attempt was made to arrest him.

For some weeks everything about camp moved along quietly, and it was hoped that further disturbance was at an end, but one afternoon while Wal was standing in front of one of the little stores that were scattered at intervals through the long main street of the town, engaged in a conversation with a lot of miners who had congregated there, a horseman came galloping up the principal thoroughfare, and halted directly in front of the door where Wal and his companions were talking.

Taking a single glance at Wal, he exclaimed, "you are the man I am looking for!" and drawing his revolver commenced shooting. He fired three shots in rapid succession, neither of which however took effect, and before he could cock his pistol again, which he was in the act of doing, Wal had "drawn a bead" on him and fired.

The ball struck him in the trigger thumb which was thereby turned, or it would have found its proper center between the eyes. Finding himself disabled, the rider put spurs to his horse and fled to the friendly shelter of the nearest ravine, but soon returned dismounted, as he discovered he had not been followed by the terrible Wal.

A crowd gathered around to shoot the wretch who had so deliberately jeopardized the lives of innocent citizens— but he called out that he was wounded and powerless and "for God sake not to kill him," that he would give himself up quietly if he could be permitted to see a doctor.

The doctor happened to be sitting in front of his office near by who took the man in, and amputated his thumb.

He was then turned over to the sheriff, who placed him

in an unoccupied log building, and appointed a guard to watch him.

During the night, however, following in the footsteps of the illustrious Wal, he eluded the vigilance of the guard, made good his escape, and ran to the mountains where he was received by his friends, who were determined to protect him from re-arrest.

The following day word was sent to the doctor to come out and dress his wounds, and obeying the summons he found him within a hundred yards of his cabin, by the side of a mining ditch, surrounded by an array of pistols, carbines and knives, determined to resist any attempt to re-arrest him.

The point selected commanded every avenue of approach up the mountain slope, without the garrison of one man being seen.

Here he remained several days, and announced to the Alcalde, through some of his friends, that he would die before giving himself up to the "Stranglers," but would submit if soldiers were sent for him.

Upon this message of defiance no further effort was made to capture him, and the town lapsed once more into its wonted quietude. Even Henderson became remarkaby docile, no further disturbances occurring between him and the miners—the trouble ending, apparently, by mutual consent.

Some months subsequent to the incidents related in the foregoing, the little camp was again thrown into a state of excitement in consequence of a report of the robbery of the mail in the cañon between Elizabethtown and Ute Creek.

It was bruited about, and proved true, that when the coach (which made tri-weekly trips between the camp and the Cimarron, to connect with the great Southern Overland Line) reached a lonely point in the cañon, where the road was narrow, and wound round a side-hill covered with a dense growth of scrubby pines, three disguised men would slip out and order the driver to halt, then without moving from their place on either side of the confined pass with their rifles pointed toward him, demand that the express box be thrown off from the boot.

This modest request being promptly complied with, they ordered the driver to move on, much to the relief of the thoroughly frightened conductor, and the two or three passengers inside.

Five or six depredations of this character were committed in the course of a month, when the people in camp began to have their suspicions aroused, and many were the conjectures as to who the guilty parties could be.

A company was formed to scour the cañon, but not even a clue of the highwaymen could be found, nor a place that exhibited any signs of a rendezvous.

This fact confirmed the suspicions of the law abiding portion of the community, that there existed in their midst and neighboring settlements at Ute Creek, an organized band of

"Road Agents" who started out only on favorable opportunities for carrying on their nefarious purposes.

It was believed by many that persons residing in Elizabethtown kept watch, and advised their partners in this crime at Ute Creek at what time a large shipment of gold would probably be made, and the number of passengers, with their names, the coach would carry.

Wal absented himself from camp a day or two at a time, and it began to be murmured that he could tell if he would, a great deal concerning these systematic robberies; and it was even hinted that he not only indirectly aided and abetted the attacks on the coach, but took an active part himself.

He was very reticent on the subject, and it was a fact commented upon by nearly every one in camp, that after an absence of two or three days, he would invariably turn up the very morning after a robbery, with a load of wood for sale, and as demurely ride through town on his little wagon as if such a thing as an attack on the coach the day before had never taken place.

Of course no positive proof of his complicity could be obtained, yet it was generally believed that he belonged to the gang.

Joe Stenson—who kept the principal saloon—and was well known throughout the Territory, not only on account of his size and weight, but also in consequence of his insatiable thirst for "bug juice" and dexterous manipulation of cards, was withal a law abiding citizen, and would tolerate nothing that was not strictly "regular" in the eye of the law. Joe wouldn't steal a horse, or carry off a red-hot stove, but woe to the unfortunate and confiding individual who sat down to Joe's game with the expectation of leaving with a cent in his clothes.

Joe's thorough knowledge of Monte, Faro, Poker and other *genteel* games, made him as much a terror behind the green-covered table as a pack of highway robbers, and while he would not hesitate to fleece some unsuspecting victim in a *gentlemanly* game, he had no sympathy with any law-breaker or "Road Agent," who would halt a man for his money without the farcical proceeding of having a little bout of cards to win it *honorably*.

One afternoon while the robberies of the mail coach were at their height, three or four broken down gamblers and loafers, sauntered into Stenson's saloon and commenced to discuss the last depredation, and the *modus operandi* of the efficient agents.

Prominent among the group was Wal; each had his theory to advance, and each expressed it freely.

Joe said, "don't yer understand,"—a favorite phrase when excited—"don't yer understand, the d——d rascals don't live a great ways from this camp, and I wouldn't wonder if a few of them—don't yer understand—are right in sight of this shebang now—don't yer understand; I hain't got no sympathy for any such work,—don't yer understand

—and would help hang every mother's son of 'em, by G—d, don't yer understand!"

Old Sam Bartlett expressed it "as his opinion, that Reub Jones, of Ute Creek knowed all about it, and was at the head of the gang."

Wal put in his oar occasionally, but from his remarks it was apparent that his sympathy was rather in favor of that style of robbing, "than *stealing it through* a d——d old Faro box."

Words waxed high and it was evident there "was going to be a *difficult*," as Kit Carson used to say.

Joe saw that trouble would ensue if the conversation was not dropped, so desirous of putting an end to it, turned to Wal and said: "Wal, we've had enough of this, so come on and have a drink and go home."

Wal accepted the invitation and with the closing remark "that he considered the robbers were a d——d sight better than some of the genteel thieves who live right in camp," he walked up to the bar, while Joe went behind and said, "Wal what will you have."

"I'll take whiskey in mine," answered Wal.

Joe set up a glass and bottle, and while mixing a toddy beneath the bar for himself, Wal seized the bottle, poured his glass full to the brim, and then deliberately emptied it on the counter with the remark: "If you don't like that, why then take your change anyway you want it," at the same instant putting his hand on his hip as if in the act of drawing his pistol.

As quick as thought, Joe knowing the desperate character of the man he had to deal with, seized a pistol from behind the bar, leveled it, fired, and Wal fell dead.

Joe immediately stepped from where he was, to the front, pistol in hand, and emptied the remaining chambers of his revolver into the prostrate form of Wal.

Joe gave himself up at once, and an examination was shortly held before the Alcalde, where all the facts were elicited, and the verdict of the jury was "Justifiable Homicide."

Thus ended the career of Wal Henderson, and his bones are now reposing on the little hill above the camp, where a score or more of others lie who have gone the same way.

CANNADY'S RANCH.

Whoever crossed the Great Plains of Kansas and Colorado in the days of the "Prairie Schooner" or lumbering stage-coach, doubtless remembers that immense tract on the confines of New Mexico, known as Maxwell's Ranch."

Lucien B. Maxwell was the companion and compeer of Kit Carson, and became famous in company with the latter as guide and hunter on the earlier exploring expeditions across the continent, particularly, that one of Fremont's in 1842-3.

Shortly after the termination of his memorable march, Maxwell married a Mexican lady, and with her became the possessor of the large grant which to-day, goes by his name. It originally comprised more than half a million acres, and is situated in one of the most charming and picturesque portions of the Rocky Mountains.

Within its area can be found the grandest peaks and cañons of that whole region, at the foot of which nestle the loveliest and most fertile valleys in the world. The Cimarron and Moreno rivers—cool mountain streams—follow the sinuosities of their tortuous passage through the towering ranges of the tract, and Ute Creek, a rushing, foaming little torrent, splashes and sparkles in the sunshine, wherever the beetling walls of the cañon that restrain its maddened waters, and the involvement of gnarled and knotted vines that overshadow it, will permit a ray of light to enter.

Thirty years ago, the whole territory of New Mexico, in which "Maxwell's Ranch" is located, was acquired by the United States under the Guadaloupe Treaty, and at that time was almost an unknown and unexplored country, except to the limited number of traders with far-off Santa Fe, and until within the last decade and a half, that portion of the mountains in which the events in our story occurred, revealed in all the grandeur and wildness of their primitiveness. But the march of civilization, in its ever-restless course westward, has completely metamorphosed the whole aspect of the country physically, and its condition socially.

Now the land is full of harvests and green meads. The mighty and seemingly interminable woods, whose mingled branches covered the immense domain with a sea of foliage, almost excluding the sun, have fallen before the axe of the pioneer. The hardy yeomen of the crowded older states, have poured in upon the footsteps of the receding savage, and the magnificent highlands and prairies, over which but a short time since deep silence brooded, except when broken by the cry of the panther and wolf, or the still more appalling yell of the Indian, is now vocal with the thousand happy sounds of a busy industry.

Where the solitary smoke of the red man's wigwam curled its thin wreath among the trees, can now be seen the dense cloud from the stamp mill, or blacksmith shop, and instead of the frail canoe, emerging quickly from a dark inlet, the flume is carried over the hills, and empties its precious waters on the rich placers below.

Our story opens in the spring of 1869, the date of which gold was discovered in the mountains and gulches of "Maxwell's Ranch." For some years previously, it was known that copper existed in the region, and several shafts had been sunk, and tunnels driven in various places. The most important of the copper lodes, and the one in fact which Maxwell worked himself, was located near the top of Old Baldy, an immense mass of disrupted granite and other primitive rocks that rises some thirteen thousand feet above the level of the sea—whose summit, bare and cold—far beyond the timber limit, gave its name.

The view from the rugged and storm-beaten crown of this grand old sentinel of the range is indescribably sublime. Far away to the north—more than ninety miles distant—the snow-capped pinnacles of the twin Spanish peaks glisten and sparkle in the sunlight, and beyond them, the majestic Pike's Peak hangs like a white cloud in the sky.

Between these, and stretching indefinitely in the purple mist, to the south and west, rugged spurs of a dozen different chains throw their shadows over the landscape. On the east the great plains of Colorado—originating at the base of the Raton range—treeless, boundless, and illimitable as the ocean, lose themselves in the deep blue of the horizon, while far away to the northeast rises the Arkansas, which like a huge silver snake twists its silent way for more than a thousand miles to discharge its mighty volume of water into the great river.

Gold was discovered early in 1867 by a party of prospectors, who were tunneling into the heart of Old Baldy in search of copper. When it became known that gold existed in paying quantities through all the mountains and gulches of the range, hundreds of miners flocked into the region, and before the end of the year had staked out their claims, and "Grouse," "Willow," "Humbug" and "Last Chance" were located, and a busy population were hard at work washing out the glittering particles of precious metal with their ong toms, cradles, sluices and hydraulics. A company was formed, and a ditch constructed forty miles in length, from the head-waters of the Little Canadian or Red rivers to supply the placers of the Moreno valley, when the water from the melting snows of Baldy range had exhausted itself.

The richest diggings were situated about half way between the Santa Fe stage-road crossing on the Cimarron, and the old Mexico town of Taos, the home of Kit Carson. At this point, on the west bank of the Moreno river, and in the very heart of the mountains, a little settlement sprung up as if by magic, and in a few months boasted of a population numbering nearly two thousand.

As in all mining camps, a most heterogeneous crowd composed the squatters in Elizabethtown, as the residents there choose to call their little city in the mountains. In its rough but busy streets you could meet the tall and plodding Yankee fresh from the low hills of New England; the active restless Texan; the jauntly-dressed commercial tourist, with his samples of bad whiskey and worse cigars; the swarthy Mexican, with his broad sombrero and scarlet sash; the darker specimen of the *genus homo*, the negro; the Heathen Chinee, the old California "forty-niners," and in fact all shades of nationalities.

Nearly every state had its representative in the motley group, who had come to seek their fortune in this new El Dorado.

It was an elegant place to study character—to learn how all the finer attributes of man can be completely crushed out by years of adversity; and how, under the same circumstances, all that is noble and pure can retain its principles untainted and incorruptible, no matter how hellish and pestilent may be its surroundings.

A characteristic of the east is formal politeness, or cool and elegant impudence; that of the far West ignorance of all etiquette and honest hospitality. The distinction is not unfavorable to men. One can easily overlook their want of what people call manners, which generally mean nothing. If they are devoid of grace, ceremony and fashion, you may more confidently depend upon the sincerity of what they say or do. One cannot but admire their broad, brawny hands; their sun-burnt honest faces; and when in company of one of these—a man perchance who will pass away from the earth absolutely unacquainted with its enervating pleasures and splendors, and free from those exciting and corrupting influences which too often deaden the feelings and warp the principles—you listen with respect to the honest phrases, and feel at once that you have fallen among friends.

There is a genuine frankness, a boldness without dissimulation, more fairness and honor in the unpolished native of the border than is usually found in an acquired politeness under the broadcloth exteriors of our populous cities in the east. Foolish grievances that disturb the order of a well-regulated town or village, often ending with a disgraceful street fight, rarely occur; an affront is seldom offered, because it is settled forever on the spot, and the revolver never drawn without accomplishing its purpose.

An understanding of this mutual code, inelegant as it may seem to those who cannot appreciate it, has founded a state of society in which a saint might live without fear of insult, but which would quickly end the career of a bully.

Occasionally bad men turn up, who run their course of "deep damnation" and become a terror to the whole country, but such men are wound up at last and "die with their boots on"—western graveyards are full of them.

Jack Cannady was one of this class, whose infernal operations in the Moreno mines, and summary death by his outraged fellow-miners is the subject of this sketch.

As has been stated, the town was located on the west

bank of the Moreno, but its pretty situation, and something of its life, must be described, to familiarize the reader with the varied character, attractions, and occupations that go to make up the aggregate of a mountain mining camp.

The timber extended from the immense bluffs behind the town almost to the edge of the river, and before a settlement could be fairly effected, the ax was called into requisition to let in the pleasant sunlight upon a portion of the slope and rich land of the intervale. Another margin of timber was confined to the banks of the stream, where, like a beautiful fringe, it followed the graceful windings of the golden water that flowed musically on in the deep shadow.

When evening approached, and the setting sun threw a flood of silvery light on the white sandstone ledge that crowned the bluffs, and the purple mist began to steal over the valley, and the dark green of the belt of timber low down on the river bottom was thrown into deeper shade as the light gradually faded away—and the crowning glory of all—when the last rays of the setting sun began their play of colors on the storm-beaten head of Old Baldy, there was presented one of the most gorgeous pictures in the world, far surpassing the storied beauty of the Italian landscape or the cold grandeur of the Alps.

Besides the magnificence of its scenery and the scale of its distances, there is an enchantment pervading the very atmosphere of the prairies and mountains, and the charm intensifies in almost every nature as each new act and new experience presents itself.

There is an indescribable quiet reigning over the actual and visible of that "far off life" which seems to touch every heart, and hardly any one who has tasted the exemption from the restraint imposed by the conventionalities of a so-called fashionable society—which the freedom of a life on the great plains or in the mountains permits—contentedly returns to an abridgement of that irrepressible *degage* within him, demanded by the crowded civilization east of the Mississippi.

The town consisted of four streets and the houses were generally of only one story, constructed of logs and adobe.

In all mining camps there is concentrated the most varied population and promiscuous occupations conceivable—from merchants and tradesmen through all the degrees of legitimate business—and from the professional faro dealer down through all the multifarious inventions for gambling, to the swindling gift enterprise on a limited scale, and three-card monte. The susceptibility of the Mexican to the charms of these games of doubtful fortune is a marked characteristic, and those people perhaps made up one-fourth of the population.

Notwithstanding such an aggregation of opposing elements, and the idleness incident to such precarious means of support, confined, too, as it was to such a comparatively limited geographical area, the discipline of the place was fair, to say the least. In fact it would have been difficult to have found a populous district in the east where better order was obtained, or where there was such an apparent disposition to obey the laws.

But, of course, it can be accounted for by the fact that the "regulations" were made by the miners themselves, each man had a voice in it, and he was bound in honor to act himself, at all times, as a guardian of the peace. Therefore, notwithstanding there were hundreds there to whose ears the shrill whistle of a bullet would sound sweeter than the soft tones of a flute, their perfect good nature and "principle of honor among thieves," kept them within reasonable bounds.

Occasionally there were desperate fights over the gambling tables in the "hells" with which the camp was filled, and sometimes a too obstreperous individual, full of "bug juice" and fight, would get a hole drilled into him by a number forty-four pistol ball, or his ribs tickled with an eleven inch bowie. Often, under the excellent skill of the doctor, these would recover, but oftener took up their last claim of six feet by two in the "bone orchard," as it was called, on the side of the mountain.

Such an intensely varied population necessarily demanded amusements as varied to satisfy the diversity of tastes aggregated there. Consequently gambling in all its seductive mutability, horse racing, the sirenizing charms of the most depraved of the *demi-monde* and the bewitching enticements of music as an accessory to these corrupting entertainments, alluringly met the ingenuous and unsuspecting among the checkered population at every footstep, some of whom, perhaps, were never before away from the virtuous influence of their rustic homes on the gentle slopes of the Texas prairies or the vine-clad hills of the older states.

From early in the evening till broad daylight next morning a concourse of musical strains floated upon the cool mountain air, ringing all the changes, from the jingling time of the "Arkansas Traveler" or "Devil's Dream" on the wheeziest of fiddles, manipulated by some negro amateur, to the choicest gems of an opera in the delicate notes of a harp.

The well disposed but sleepily inclined citizen could select his lullaby from them, as it suited his fancy, for all through the night it was unflaggingly kept up. Nor did it cease when the sun cast his long rays on the little valley next day, but in the brightest hours the same weary round of tune continued, where in the shade of big trees and the retirement of the gambling "hells" and drinking saloons, the doubtful harmony might be heard enticing the unsophisticated to the mysteries of their interiors.

Occasionally this enchantment of sweet melody was accompanied with the coarse language of some lascivious song by a rough balladist, who was chorused by a dozen discordant voices gathered around a magic center, or the shuffling sound of huge feet kept time to the quick movement of an inspiring jig.

The average miner would come into town as often as two or three times a week, and if fortunate in his diggings would make for the first gaming table, to indulge in his favorite Mexican monte. Winning, he would decorate himself with an enormous stock of flash jewelry, harnessing his neck with a watch chain three or four yards long, and thus glitteringly attired "would make the rounds," stopping at every saloon to treat the crowd, or kick up a fuss with the first man that got in his way. Losing—generally the rule—he went drunk and sulkily back to his claim, consoling himself with the hope of better success next time. And so the majority of lives were passed—not a few "died with their boots on" in some drunken quarrel with their friends to whom they had offered a real or fancied insult.

Cannady was a tall, angular, villainous-looking specimen of humanity, who was born in Missouri, but whose fiendish acts in the Kansas free state struggles, had forced him to become an outlaw in the mountains of New Mexico, where, in one of their deep defiles, he squatted himself and married a native woman. Surly and reticent, usually, but pugnacious as a bull-dog when drunk, he always managed to kick up a row whenever he came into camp, and as certainly returned home with his head bandaged up, the result of encounters he had provoked in his midnight orgies around the town, or in quarrels over the gambling table.

Cannady's Ranch was located at the entrance to Taos cañon, about seventeen miles from the mining camp of Elizabethtown, on the main trail to Taos, to which it was nearly the same distance.

The spot Cannady had selected for his retreat was well calculated as a fit field for his diabolical deeds, notwithstanding the charm of its magnificent scenery. But of course i was not on account of any latent æsthetic sentiment of his nature that led him to choose this picturesquely beautiful nook in the mountains—it was because of its retirement and loneliness—where he could operate boldly, with the chances of discovery reduced to the minimum of possibility.

The unbroken wall of the cañon rises abruptly for over a thousand feet on one side, where under its dark veil of shade the cabin stood, and at the opposite side, scarcely three hundred feet away, a corresponding mass of rock shoots upward to nearly the same height, forming the other wall.

This fearful gap in the range was made untold ages ago by one of those terrible convulsions of nature, the effects of which are visible on every hand in the Rocky Mountains; for it can plainly be seen that the walls of the cañon were originally closed, and what was once merely a huge fissure, time and erosion have worn into a respectable passage through the giant barrier.

The entrance to the cañon and its surroundings was a perfect wilderness of beauty. Little springs gushed out from the base of the tall granite cliffs that stood like towers amidst the dwarfed oaks nodding around them, and the babbling little rills as they trickled slowly over the smooth pebbles, sent up the music of their tuneful waters in sweet concert with the ever whispering pines.

At all seasons and for all hearts, forest scenery has a charm, and how, under the very mantle of such a gorgeous landscape, man can commit the most horrid crimes seems a mystery.

Cannady's cabin, with its bloody history, was the only object that clashed with the loveliness of its embosomment; it was constructed in the rudest style of back-woods architecture—of unhewn logs placed together at the ends, after the manner in which children build their houses of corn-cobs—and the interstices chinked up with mud. It had only three windows, and the door was formed out of a few pine shingles or rough clapboards, fastened together with wooden pins and hung on hinges of the same material. The roof was composed of similar riven clapboards, which were kept in their place by long and heavy logs, laid lengthwise of the building at short intervals from each other, and over the whole, a mass of dirt some two feet thick was deposited. The floor of this hut, like all the houses in New Mexico, of the poor, was of earth, and the fire-place of the same substance.

Cannady's family consisted of his wife and his father-in-law, who both lived in constant dread of him and one child, which he afterward killed.

The old Mexican, his father-in-law, had cleared a little garden-patch around the cabin, where he and his daughter raised a few onions, sweet potatoes and melons, but Cannady's ostensible occupation was that of a sort of inn-keeper, where travelers on their way to Taos could get a drink of the villain ous compound sold in that region, under the name of liquor, or feed their animals while they smoked a poor cigar or a pipe full of worse tobacco.

At times Cannady would make his appearence in camp with large amounts of money, causing considerable speculation among the honest miners and the gamblers, where an how he had raised such a "stake." If such hints were thrown out in his presence, or if he was directly asked the question by some one bolder than the rest, his reply was invariably, "I've been up to Taos, damn you, and win it, is it any o' your business?"

During the intensely exciting times of prospecting through the different ranges for quartz leads in the early weeks of the discovery of gold and silver in that region, two young Indians one morning brought down to Maxwell, a gunny sack half full of gold-bearing rock, which they told him they found beyond Cannady's ranch in the lower end of the Taos range.

Maxwell, anxious to develop the matter, and eager to obtain more specimens, furnished the boys with animals and provisions to secure undoubted proof of what he considered a "rich strike."

The Indians set out on their journey of discovery early the next morning, and when they came to the mouth of the cañon where Cannady lived, they separated, one taking a short cut over the mountains by the trail, and the other going up the cañon to Cannady's for water. They were to have met two miles beyond, in the cañon, west of the ranch, but they never saw each other again.

Two days afterward, the mule which the boy rode who had gone to Cannady's, was found in the Cimarron cañon all alone, browsing on his way back to Maxwell's. No trace of the missing boy could be found, and the tribe to which he belonged, and who were friendly to the whites, declared that he had been murdered by some Americans.

Maxwell, upon whom the whole Ute nation looked as their father, endeavored to talk them out of what he considered a ridiculous idea, but he could not remove the impression from their minds.

Nearly two months had elapsed and the matter had almost ceased to receive any more thought, when, one afternoon, two miners of Elizabethtown, on their way back from Taos, on approaching Cannady's ranch—who happened to be away at the time—discovered a half starved Mexican dog tugging and pulling at something he had evidently unearthed a short distance from the rear of the cabin.

Curiosity led them to dismount, tie their mules and investigate what the cur was apparently so interested in. Their examination showed it to be the leg of a human being, and on further search, discovered the body of the Indian boy with his skull split open as if done with an axe.

The news of the discovery of the murder of the missing Ute was imparted to only a few of the best citizens of Elizabethtown, who immediately took measures for the arrest of

Cannady, knowing that if the Indians discovered it, they would break out and probably massacre the whole settlement. Cannady was taken by surprise one morning and brought to town before the Alcalde. But meanwhile, some way or other, the Indians became aware of the facts, and it was only through the good counsels of Maxwell they were finally bought off, and a terrible slaughter prevented. When the Indians were made acquainted with the tragic fate of the boy of their tribe, and knew that he had been brutally murdered by the desperado Cannady, they declared their determination of avenging his death. Maxwell, fearing that some innocent white man would be killed, whom their roving bands might mistake for Cannady, resolved to effect an amicable settlement of the affair if possible, rather than that the chief should give the order to his warriors to hunt for Cannady.

The excellent counsel of Maxwell prevailed, and the Indians were pacified by his presenting each of the boy's immediate relations with a pony, and the citizens of Elizabethtown contributing money, provisions and ammunition. Thus, through Maxwell's perfect knowledge of the Indian character, and his timely intervention, a war with one of the most powerful tribes was averted, for the Indians had fully made up their minds to put on their war-paint, and first of all, in their contemplated depredations, threatened to kill every white man in the mines. Maxwell did not hesitate, however, to tell the chief with whom he made arrangements, that if any of them ever came across Cannady, and they were sure of their man, no trouble would ensue "if they killed him right in his tracks."

In the course of Cannady's examination before the Alcalde in town, some of the facts in relation to the boy's death were elicited from Cannady's Mexican wife. She stated that the young Indian had called at the ranch, and that her husband was out in the hills somewhere with his rifle, temporarily; that she gave the boy a bowl of coffee to drink, and while peaceably sitting enjoying her proffered refreshment, the bloodthirsty man slipped in quietly behind him, holding in his hand a hatchet, with which he struck him in the head two or three times, cleaving his skull and killing him instantly. He then took him by the heels, dragged him a few rods in the rear of the house, and there buried him, where his body was discovered by the prowling, half starved cur.

There were no organized courts in that particular region, and the result was that Cannady was released, and returned with the woman to the ranch. Policy, perhaps, dictated this course, which, under all the circumstances—too complicated to be explained in this sketch—was the best at the time.

After Cannady had returned to the ranch, and there was no longer anything to fear from the Indians, nothing disturbed the usual tranquillity of the camp into which daily new adventurers thronged and new business opened, as the requirements of the bustling little place demanded f r nearly three months after the murder of the Ute boy. Then, early one afternoon, Cannady rode into camp in the greatest excitement, announcing that he had found the dead body of some unknown man, lying on the trail near his ranch, shot through the heart, and, scattered around in every direction, a considerable amount of fractional currency—that he had left him just as he had discovered him, and had hurried into town to give the alarm—stating, in his opinion, that hostile Indians had done the work, and advising that a mounted party be formed to scour around the mountains in the vicinity of the cañon to follow up the trail if possible.

The camp was all impatience and restlessness under the news, and in less than an hour, twenty-three men were mounted, well armed, and with three day's rations, were on their way to the Taos range with Cannady as their guide. Reaching the ranch in a short time they found the body of the murdered man as Cannady had described, who was immediately recognized as Billy Edwards, well known through the mines as an industrious, prospering miner, quiet, orderly and respected by all who knew him. Only a few days previously he had sold out his claim, and purchasing a pack animal had started for Santa Fe *via* Taos, with all he possessed in the world secured about his person and on the back of his little "burro."

The appearance of his body and the money scattered around him all led to the confirmation of Cannady's story, and expressed suspicions that the Indians had killed him. No one in the crowd for a moment thought of implicating Cannady in the affair—in fact, he appeared as eager as any to trace the murder to its author, and make an extended scout among the hills. Three days were spent by the party in fruitless search for some trace of Indians, but not a sign could be discovered, and they returned to the camp with the remains of the unfortunate Edwards, and buried them in the little hill just north of the town, already dotted over with the graves of many murdered men. The matter was not dropped but talked over constantly, for Edwards was beloved by every one. Little knots of miners and mountaineers could be seen almost any time around the stores and saloons discussing the question of the murder, and each advancing his own theory of how "poor Billy" was surprised and killed.

Now and then some would hint that Cannady knew more about the killing than many supposed he did. One, who was more emphatic in his assertions than others, declared most decidedly at a discussion in the hotel over the affair: "To be sure nobody knows what Cannady's been about, but it isn't honest people that do what they have to do in the dark; he always has oceans of cash, and now where does he get it; that's what I want to know?"

It was only a few days afterward that some prospectors, who had come down to the mines from Taos, stated that Cannady had just been up there on a terrible spree, and had lots of money, which he used freely in drinking and gambling. So, immediately upon this news, the two miners who had intimated more strongly than the others that Cannady could tell more about Edwards death than any one else, started for his ranch one evening without letting any of the rest of the camp know of their expedition. When they reached the place they found it vacated, as they supposed it would be, as it was Cannady's custom whenever he left for Taos or Elizabethtown to shut up his cabin and send his wife and father-in-law to some of their relatives to stay during his absence.

The two men determined to take advantage of this aspect of affairs, and make a thorough investigation of the ranch and its surroundings to discover if possible some foundation for the conjectures they had formed of Cannady's mode of life, and his murderous proclivities as they believed. A short distance from the ranch, and just inside a little clump of thick timber, the remains of a recent fire were found, and in stirring over the pile of ashes a lot of partly charred bones were exposed, which they carefully collected and put in a sack. Not far off another heap of ashes was discovered, and a similar collection of bones were made.

On entering the cabin, which they now no longer had any hesitancy in doing, they found in the corner of the room used as a kitchen, a spot where the dirt-floor yielded under the pressure of their feet, and which looked as if it had been recently disturbed. Taking a spade that hung on a peg in the wall, they dug down about two feet, and unearthed the mutilated fragments of a human body.

Putting a portion of the remains in a sack, they care

fully replaced the dirt, so that the floor appeared as they had found it, and returned to camp with the sack of bones.

The result of their trip was disclosed to only a few, and a secret meeting was held the same evening to devise the best measure to capture Cannady—whose hellish-life was now manifest—before he became alarmed and escaped out of the country.

The next morning, learning from some parties who had just passed the ranch that Cannady had returned, it was decided that not a momont should be lost in the attempt to secure the murderous villain, and accordingly it was planned that ten picked men should start immediately for his den, but instead of going directly to his door, should keep past his cabin, singing and laughing and appear generally jolly, as if they were only bent on a spreeing trip to Taos, while he, no doubt, observing that the crowd were not going to halt, would make his appearance and call them back.

The proposition was immediately acted upon, and the ruse worked perfectly, for no sooner had they come within a hundred yards of the ranch, and were, to all appearance, going by, than Cannady came outside and hailed them with "Hello fellows," ain't you going to stop? Where are you bound?"

The party held a brief consultation, apparently further to carry out their plan, and then one of them called out: "Got anything to drink in there, Cannady?"

"Yes," he replied, "lots of it? come in."

"Say we do, boys," said the first speaker; and they all turned toward the house, dismounted, and hitched their horses to the trees outside.

No sooner had they all entered than a break was made for Cannady, and in a moment half a dozen revolvers were pulled out of their belts, and "they had the drop on him." Their business was explained in a very few words, they told him what they knew—and if he made a move, they would "blow the top of his head off."

He was bound hand and foot with a couple of lariat ropes, and tossed into a wagon that the party had brought with them, but which, until they wanted it, remained out of sight down the trail. His Mexican wife and father-in-law were also taken to town as witnesses.

As soon as they reached the camp, Cannady was first heavily shackled at the blacksmith shop, and then lodged in a little log building, improvised as a jail, which was guarded by two plucky miners.

For two or three days the ranch was searched for the purpose of making further discoveries in Cannady's bloody work, and before a week had passed, the remains of seventeen bodies were found buried inside and outside the cabin. Charred fragments of skeletons were hidden in various places in the vicinity, and it was supposed that many others besides those whose bones were found, had been murdered by Cannady, and left in the mountains just where he had killed them, and were eaten by the wolves.

Frequently miners would leave for other portions of the territory, to be absent only a few days, but nothing was ever heard of them afterward. They probably never got beyond Cannady's ranch, where they stopped for a drink, or to rest for a few moments, only to be killed and robbed by that mountain assassin.

How many a mother, or young wife has suddenly ceased to hear from an adventurous son, or husband, who was seeking his fortune in the "far west," and whose fate was to become the victim of such fiends in human shape as Cannady, will never be known, for their number is one of the horrid secrets that is buried in the grave with them and their murderer. Perhaps some, under whose eyes these facts may fall, will find a possible reason for the protracted absence of one who has been looked for for years, but who will never come.

After the horrid developments at the ranch, threats were made by the exasperated miners to lynch Cannady at once, but they finally determined that he should have a fair and impartial trial, by a jury of twelve men, to be selected by himself; that a judge should be selected by the crowd; he to appoint a prosecuting attorney and counsel for the defense.

As soon as it was agreed in camp to give Cannady a chance for his life, the "fandango hall" of Joe Stenson's "Miner's Saloon," was selected as the court room, and the trial set for eight o'clock that evening.

At the hour appointed the crowd began to gather, and in a little while the room was packed with as motley and as hard a looking mob as ever got together in the West. It was a curious mixture of ignorance, manhood, vice, virtue and villainy. Some of the truest men that ever lived stood in that dimly-lighted little black room; and some hearts were here too, as deeply-dyed—if the truth were known as Cannady's. Miners, merchants, gamblers and Mexicans were mixed promiscuously, and the determined faces, and show of revolvers spoke plainly enough, "there wasn't going to be any fooling" in the matter. The red light of a blazing fire, made of dry pine knots, nearly as combustible as powder, shot up the dark chimney-place in the corner, throwing a glimmering and confused mist over the brindled crowd assembled there, and the fitful glimmer of three or four untrimmed kerosene lamps, threw weird shadows on the whitewashed walls, as if the ghosts of the murderer's victims had come to be phantom witnesses of his agony and bitterness.

Tom Pollock, an excellent citizen and veteran miner, was unanimously chosen judge, and Cannady, of course, had the good sense to pick his jury from the very best element in the place. The prosecuting attorney was a young lawyer who happened to be in the camp, and a young man, assessor of internal revenue at the time, volunteered to defend the case, whose offer was readily accepted by both the judge and Cannady.

The preliminaries being now all arranged, the prisoner

was brought in by his guards, seated on a cracker box in front of the jury, and by the side of his youthful counsel and only friend in the whole crowd.

There were the usual oaths administered, every man understanding perfectly his position, and acting upon the fearful responsibility demanded by the situation of affairs in that isolated region, and the necessity of summary justice, no matter on whose head it might fall.

In a few pithy sentences, Judge Pollock told Cannady the object of their gathering, and reviewed the terrible crimes that had been traced to his den. He pointed to the ghastly remains and charred fragments of human skeletons that lay piled upon a rude pine table before him, which had been dug up inside of his ranch, and in the timber in its vicinity, and asked him how he could look upon that loathsome and horrid sight, without expecting the vengeance of God to strike him dead in his tracks. The Judge grew almost eloquent in his recitation of Cannady's damnable deeds, and a death-like stillness pervaded the place, as the words fell hot and earnestly from his lips, broken only by the convulsive click of a revolver now and then when the excitement intensified; and, but for the sound advice to "give the miserable wretch a square deal," the trial would have ended right there.

When the Judge had finished, Cannady, whose cheeks were ashen pale, his eyes distended and tearless, riveted his gaze on the determined men before him, utterly at a loss what to do or say, and distracted alternately by hope and fear, for he felt the enormity of his guilt, and knew in his cowardly heart he deserved death right then, without the least show of mercy.

The prosecuting attorney stated, in opening the case, that he had not much to say, and only referred to the manner in which Cannady selected his victims, and the extreme caution he had always exercised to avoid murdering well-known residents of the camp; understanding perfectly their sudden disappearance from the community would excite suspicion and lead to an exhaustive search of their whereabouts. He showed how Cannady had always singled out for the consummation of his diabolical ends some poor miner who, perhaps, had only a nick-name—alone and penniless, *en route* for some other portions of the country; some isolated, reticent man, who seldom or never held much communication with others in the camp. That he was too cowardly to kill a well-known merchant or citizen of the town—all of these could pass a night securely at his ranch; to them he would extend a rough, generous hospitality, and at the same time endeavor to impress upon their minds the danger of a trip through the mountains without an escort; that the Indians were treacherous, and prowling over the hills constantly; besides there were numbers of outlaws and highwaymen, who sought the solitude of the mountain fastnesses to murder and rob; that he would tell them of his own marvelous escapes and terrible hand-to-hand encounters with desperadoes, all for the effect it might have in drawing suspicion from himself; that those whom he would gladly have killed he did not dare to, and they only had been saved from the clutches of this bloodthirsty terror of the mountains by the very cowardice of his nature. He scathed Cannady fearfully, working up a more exasperated feeling if possible than before against him, and then called in his witnesses.

The doctor was the first to testify, and his evidence, confined to the character of the charred bones, settled any question as to the possibility of their not being those of human beings.

The two miners, who had made the horrid discoveries at the ranch, then related to the jury their simple story, describing accurately on a plain board, with a piece of burnt stick the location of the cabin, its surroundings, and the position of the ash heaps. They made a graphic if not artistic sketch, with their rude pencil, and its effect upon the crowd and the jury was manifested by expressions addressed indirectly to Cannady more emphatic than elegant, but which the judge in a few moments succeeded in suppressing.

Antonio Montoyo—Cannady's Mexican father-in-law—who could speak nothing but Spanish, was questioned through an interpreter, and his plain recital of what he had seen left no possible hope for Cannady. He told his story of one cold blooded murder he had witnessed as follows: "One evening a stranger came to the ranch and wanted to stay all night; he was put in the same room with me, where I was lying on the floor. After the stranger was fast asleep, Cannady cautiously entered the room with a candle in one hand and a revolver in the other. I was wide awake at the time but did not dare to speak. Cannady then softly approached the bed on which the stranger lay, and who was sound asleep, put the muzzle of the pistol against his left temple and fired. The murdered man never moved or made a sound, and I jumped up, when Cannady threatened to serve me the same way if ever I breathed a word of what I had seen. Cannady then ordered me to hold the light while he examined the wound. The man was large, and had a long red beard; there was a small hole in his temple, and one in the back of his head. I was afraid he would kill me, and when he told me to go and bring him a bucket of water, I ran up the cañon and did not stop until I reached Taos. I never knew what he did with the body, and he never spoke to me about the murder afterward."

Cannady's wife, a young Mexican girl, apparently too youthful for either wife or mother, was called, and through the interpreter stated that she had witnessed a number of murders at the ranch, but had been afraid to say a word, because Cannady always swore he would kill her if she did; but when he murdered her child in the most cruel and atrocious manner right before her eyes, she made up her mind that she would expose his bloody life as soon as she could find a safe opportunity.

Her testimony was clear and distinct, and she exhibited no trace of emotion as she gazed with her girlish face upon her cold-blooded husband, who cowed before her dark eyes.

A host of others gave in their evidence, all implicating Cannady directly or indirectly with a whole series of butcheries, and whose unanimous opinion was "that he deserved the death of a dog."

Cannady had no witnesses to offer in his defense, but made a rambling incoherent sort of a speech, in which, of course, he denied all the terrible crimes that had been imputed to him, acknowledging only the murder of the Ute boy, whom, he had declared, he had killed in self-defense to save his family.

Every word the hardened wretch uttered, however, had only tended to confirm the minds of the jury and the others present of his guilt, and after half an hour of successive contradictions and weak argument, he sat down.

The prosecuting attorney submitted the fate of the accused to the jury without discussing the points of the case; he felt it would only be consuming valuable time, and if there was anything to be said, let the defense offer it.

The counsel for the defense, though in his own mind convinced of the deep-dyed villainy of his brutal client, felt it incumbent upon him to make an appeal in his behalf, which he did so eloquently, and built up hypotheses so rapidly that some of the rougher element, afraid that his efforts might be effectual, became rather demonstrative and crowded around him in a somewhat too serious manner, but were quieted b a few positive words from the judge—a rather decided but not particularly pleasant compliment to his forensic ability.

The judge made another one of his significant addresses in his charge in submitting the case to the jury, reminding them that if their verdict should be unanimous, according to the secret arrangement, Cannady would be executed immediately after they had returned it in front of the saloon in which the trial was held, but if a single dissenting vote was cast, he should be remanded to jail, and await a regular trial at the next term of the district court, at Taos.

It was midnight when the fate of Cannady was given to the twelve men whom he himself had chosen, and for an hour they deliberated upon the question of summary punishment, when they stood eleven for death, and one for a regular trial according to law.

They so reported, and that one dissenting vote saved Cannady's life that night, and he was locked up in the little log jail again, doubly shackled, and guarded by an additional force.

The crowd sulkily submitted to the decision, but a good many threats were muttered about "getting even with him," "having his heart's blood," etc. The excitement subsided, however, in the morning, and the camp gradually resumed its normal condition.

Four or five days after the midnight trial in "Stensons' saloon" another prospecting party, just in from the mountains, rode into town with the head of the unfortunate victim so accurately described by the Mexican father-in-law of Cannady in his evidence before the court.

There was the "hole in the left temple," and the other "in the back of the head." The features were considerably decomposed, but long masses of sandy beard still adhered to the face, and the remains were at once recognized as those of Major Over, formerly from Ohio, who had left the mines at the time of his murder for Santa Fe.

This confirmatory proof of Cannady's atrocities aroused the indignation of the people again—which was only slumbering, and another secret meeting was called.

A little after midnight, the hour agreed upon, about twenty determined men met in the back of one of the little log stores, heavily armed, and their faces disguised with masks improvised for the occasion.

The dingy looking place was lighted by a few tallow-candles that shed a dim, sallow haziness over the piles of bacon, kegs of powder, picks, shovels, and other miner's goods, which were stored there, and upon the strange looking faces assembled to mete out that justice which they believed had been too long delayed.

The doctor who resided in the camp, had been invited to be present, and was there, not to exercise an active part in the summary vengence about to take place, but rather for the purpose of drawing out some information from the doomed man at the place of execution concerning those whom he had murdered, in order that relatives or friends might be informed of the time and manner of their death, and the fate of the murderer.

After half an hour spent in discussion relative to a plan of operations, finally it was agreed that the party should meet at the same hour the next night just outside the camp, at the Taos trail crossing of Ute creek, from there go to the jail, take Cannady out and hang him.

After these preliminaries had been arranged a solemn oath was sworn to carry out their plans, and the little assembly broke up to come together again on the following night at the appointed rendezvous.

Nothing disturbed the usual routine of the camp next day, and not a suspicion was entertained that Cannady was so soon to meet the tragic fate he richly deserved.

The hours dragged their weary length along, and the determined men who had sworn to avenge the horrible butcheries of Cannady were impatient for night to come that their work might be consummated.

Anon the evening came, walking noiselessly over the mountains. The clouds that had hung over the valley all day like a pall, broke apart in painted masses, and behind their tinseled fragments the blazing sun with broadened disc, lingered in the west for a few moments, shedding a rich and shifting radiance over the landscape, which soon faded into the deep eventide as the day-light sank behind the hills that overshadowed the town.

The pines, the valley, the foaming torrent, and the little

camp all retired from view as if they wished to go to sleep beneath the friendly shadows.

Calm and beautiful with troops of stars overhead, a deep and reverent silence stole over the place as if the justice of Heaven looked down upon the act that was to be committed, when the men who had sworn to keep their pledges marched out silently into the night, and met at Ute creek ford.

Consulting together for a few moments under the trees on the bank, their plans were hastily formed and put into operation at once.

Reaching the vicinity of the rude log jail, they stopped to reconnoiter, and finding everything quiet, four of them went up to the door and knocked.

The summons was promptly answered, and as soon as the door swung open in rushed the masked men, who overpowered the guard and disarmed them in a moment.

Cannady was bound hand and foot, tied on a litter that the party had improvised at the creek, and without a whisper they took up their line of march for the place of execution.

Three quarters of a mile away, through a deep cañon in the hills, was a little opening where a corral and a slaughter pen had been constructed in which the cattle used by the miners were killed. Here in the forks of two contiguous trees an unhewn portion of another was laid.

In one end of this transverse stick holes had been bored, and four stout pieces of timber about three inches thick and ten feet long inserted, which served as a rough wheel and axle, upon which the dead beeves were hoisted—now to be turned into a scaffold!

To this lonely spot the murderer and his excutioners journeyed on their silent expedition.

Nothing broke the almost painful stillness as the unflinching little procession marched under the hushed shadows of the mountains piled up into the calm firmanent above them, until they reached the opening where the slaughter pen stood.

Then, suddenly the dismal cry of a pack of wolves reverberated through the hills, as driven by the approaching tramp of feet from their midnight feast of half-dried hides, they stole to the edge of the timber.

But soon their horrid howls grew more distant, melted away, and deep silence brooded over the scene again. The masked men then formed a semicircle around the doomed man, lighted torches that they had brought with them, and commenced their horrid work.

Cannady with his arms and ankles tied and heavily ironed, sat crouching on the blood-stained floor of the slaughter pen, while the sickly light from the torches glared upon the disguised faces of his executioners and his shaggy hair, adding still more horror to the strange scene.

The doctor, the only one beside the prisoner unarmed and without disguise, then stepped in front of Cannady, who in trembling voice asked him what all this meant.

The doctor said to him that he ought to understand by

this time from the preparation that had been made, and the determined course that had been pursued by those who had brought him there, that his stay on this earth was of short duration.

He said to the miserable wretch: "After a fair and impartial trial, and the discovery of overwhelming proofs of your murderous course, you are about to expiate the foul and unwarrantable crimes of which you have been adjudged guilty.

"I come to you not as one of your executioners, but to learn if possible during the last moments of your life the names of your unknown victims, whose scattered bones and ghastly skeletons only have been found.

"I come for the purpose of hearing your confession before you are launched into eternity to meet your God.

"Of those known to have been killed by your hands I desire first of all to know about, Edwards, who was found murdered by the trail near your ranch. What have you to say in relation to that?"

"As God is my judge," replied Cannady, "I never laid eyes on Edwards until I found him dead, with the currency scattered around him just as I reported it in camp."

"Where did you hide the remains of California Joe, who left the mines and was never seen after he entered the Taos cañon?" continued the doctor in his inquiries.

"The last time I saw Joe," Cannady said "was when

he passed my ranch on his way to the Burro Mountains, and I don't know where he is."

The doctor then asked him some questions in relation to the sudden disappearance of Major Over, but Cannady, who had learned nothing of the fact that the head of the unfortunate Major had been found buried under the floor of his cabin, answered that he had never seen Over after he left his ranch early one afternoon for Santa Fe. "I have no idea of his whereabouts," said Cannady to the doctor's pressing questions. "He probably is in the mountains somewhere, murdered by the Apaches, for all I know."

Thus the hardened wretch continued to lie as the interrogatories were pressed upon him, and no appeal was strong enough to draw out a single word of confession, and any hope of information was abandoned, so the doctor left him in disgust.

All the preparations being in readiness for the final act of the tragic scene, Cannady was lifted upon a rude platform under the beam stretching between the two trees, where he sat for a moment crouching and trembling, now fully understanding the horrible death that awaited him, when, with a kick and the terse phrase, "stand up you murdering hound," one of his executioners helped him to his feet. The rope was now secured to the beam, and the noose placed around Cannady's neck. In the next instant three of the stoutest men in the party seized him and threw him bodily fully five feet into the air, and, being a man of huge frame, as he came back on the end of the rope with his whole weight, his death was almost instantaneous.

The torches were immediately extinguished, and the crowd quickly dispersed, leaving the body of Cannady dangling from the windlass in the deserted slaughter pen.

Early the next morning, just as the sun began to peep over the towering heights of Baldy range and flood the little valley with its golden light, some one who happened to ride into town from the direction of the cañon where the lynching had taken place, saw the body of Cannady, and in a few moments the little camp was all astir, as the news of Cannady's execution was heralded through the mountains and gulches.

Soon crowds were wending their way up the cañon to the old slaughter pen, where the body of the murderer still remained unmolested, hanging too high to be reached by the wolves who had evidently been prowling around him during the night.

The Alcalde made his appearance, and immediately summoned a jury from those present, examined one or two persons to find out something about the affair, but all without eliciting a single fact.

He then ordered the body cut down, and the doctor to examine it, who stated that death was "caused by complete dislocation of the cervical vertebræ."

The guards at the jail swore they did not hear a word spoken when Cannady was forcibly taken from them, and they could not recognize a single one of the party on account of their perfect disguise.

The jury retired for a few moments, and, after a short deliberation, returned the verdict, "that Cannady came to his death by hanging, which was done by some person or persons unknown."

An application was then made by the doctor for the body for examination, he promising to bury it without expense to the town if his request should be granted.

Upon this the Alcalde called out to the crowd, "All those in favor of letting the doctor have the murderer's remains for scientific examination will manifest it by saying aye?" A universal shout of affirmation rang through the hills in response to the Alcalde's question. Contrary minded, no, cried the Alcalde. A solitary "no" was uttered by a miner who sat on the top rail of the cattle-corral fence, swinging his long legs and pulling vigorously at a corn-cob pipe.

"What's you objection Bill," said the Alcalde.

"I want to see a rope tied around the legs of the d—d villain, and help drag him to the mountain near his ranch and leave him there for the coyotes to finish him up," replied Bill.

This created a ripple of merriment, but the doctor secured the remains of Cannady, sent them to his office, preserving the murderer's skull, which he kept on the shelf, and the remnant of the dissected body he placed in a rough pine box, and buried in a grove on a little hill overlooking the camp, near, but not by the side of the murderer's victims.

Thus ended the career of one of the most bloodthirsty villains that ever lived in the mountains of New Mexico. The deity whom he worshiped asked blood, and blood he gave him by a whole hecatomb of human lives. The justice he merited was meted out to him, to the great relief and satisfaction of the whole community.

GENERAL FORSYTH'S FIGHT ON THE "ARRIC-KAREE FORK" OF THE REPUBLICAN.

A DESPERATE CHAPTER IN KANSAS HISTORY.

I was sitting in my office at Fort Harker, on a warm evening in the latter part of September, 1868, musing, over a pipe full of "Lone Jack," upon the possible extent of the impending Indian war, (which had already been planned by General Sheridan, in the seclusion of my own quarters only the night before). It was rapidly growing dark; the somber line of the twilight curve had almost met the western horizon, and only the faintest tinge of purple beneath, marked the intermedium between the gloaming and the inkiness of the rayless sky.

Nothing disturbed my reverie—as I wandered in imagination over the bleak expanse of the Arkansas, Cimarron and Canadian rivers, so soon to be the scene of active operations, except the monotonous clicking of the relay in the window of the next room, where the government night operator was on duty, who too was meditating in the darkness.

The terrible massacre on Spillman Creek, only a few weeks before, still furnished food for revengeful thoughts that would not down, as images of the murdered women and little ones rose in horrible visions upon the thick night before me.

The dismal howl of a hungry wolf, borne upon the still air from the timbered recesses of the "Smoky," but added to the weird aspect that my surroundings were hurriedly assuming, and there seemed some portentous and indescribable *thing* bearing down upon the place.

Suddenly the operator—while the clicking of the instruments became more nervous and varied from their monotone of the whole evening—exclaimed: "My God! Major, what's this?" What is what? said I, jumping from my chair and rushing to his side.

Quickly lighting his little lamp and seizing his pencil, he wrote upon a blank, as I looked over his shoulder, and read—while the clicking grew more convulsive still—these words: * * * "General Forsyth surrounded by Indians on the Republican; Lieut. Beecher, the Doctor and many of the scouts killed—nearly the entire command, including the General, wounded. Stillwell, one of the scouts, run the gauntlet of the savages and brings this report. Col. Carpenter, 10th Cavalry, and his command leave immediately to relieve them." * * * * * *

This was a fragment of the whole dispatch going over the wires from Fort Hayes to Fort Leavenworth and Washington, and we had taken enough of it to know that a terrible disaster had befallen the gallant Forsyth, of Sheridan's staff, and his plucky band of scouts—all civilians and Kansans.

The story of this fight—in many respects one of the most remarkable and desperate in the annals of our Indian wars—is particularly interesting now, since the State, in its wisdom, has established on a firm foundation, a Historical Society, in the archives of which are recorded the struggles of her settlement, whose chronicles make up a large and intensely thrilling portion of our American classics.

While the Headquarters of General Sheridan—who was, at the date of this narrative, in command of the Department of the Missouri—were temporarily established at Fort Harker, where he was consummating his arrangements for a winter campaign against the hostile tribes, the idea suggested itself to him that a body of carefully selected men, composed of the best material to be found on the frontier, under the leadership of an experienced officer could effect excellent results. These scouts, as they were to be termed, were to go anywhere, and act entirely independent of the regularly organized troops about to take the field.

Generals Custer and Sully—the next in rank to Sheridan, and both already famous as Indian fighters—coincided with this view of the Commanding General, and it was determined to equip fifty picked frontiersmen at once and commission Forsyth as their leader, who had, in the incipiency of the thing, modestly solicited the responsible position.

The fifty men were chosen from an aggregate of more

than two thousand employed by the Government in various positions at Forts Harker and Hays, and the reader may rest assured that only those were accepted who possessed the essential qualifications of indomitable courage, wonderful endurance, perfect marksmanship, and a knowledge of the Indian character.

General Forsyth chose for his Lieutenant his particular friend, F. H. Beecher, of the 3d Infantry, a nephew of the celebrated Brooklyn preacher.

Some days were occupied at Fort Harker in fitting out the little expedition, but no unnecessary equipage or superfluous camp paraphernalia formed any part of the supplies.

There were no tents or wagons; pack mules carried the commissary stores, which were of the simplest character, and as the object of the party was *war* its *impedimenta* were reduced to the minimum.

Each man was mounted on an excellent horse and his armament consisted of a breech-loading rifle and two revolvers.

This troop of brave men left Harker for Hays in the latter part of August, from which point their arduous duties were commenced.

On the 29th of that month all the preliminaries for taking the field having been completed, and their surgeon having joined (whose name I have unfortunately forgotten), they marched out of the Fort, and after scouting over a large area for several days without meeting any signs of the Cheyennes, they concluded to go to Wallace to recuperate and refit.

Some time during the second week in September, the Indians made a raid on a government wagon train a short distance from a tank station on the Kansas Pacific Railroad about a hundred miles beyond Wallace, and as soon as the news reached the Fort, over the wires, Forsyth and his little band of scouts started to intercept the savages on their retreat.

The next morning the scouts struck the fresh trail of the Indians, and by forced marches came so close to them that they compelled them to split into insignificant detachments, and night coming rapidly on the General lost the trail. The conclusion was, after a consultation with the best plainsmen among the party, that the Indians would naturally go northward, so it was determined to take that direction in pursuit.

The scouts continued their course for more than a week without the most trifling incident to relieve the wearisome monotony of the march, until suddenly on the afternoon of the eighth day, as they were approaching the bluffs of the Republican river, they discovered an immense trail still leading to the North.

The signs indicated that a large body of warriors, with pack animals, women and children, and lodges of a big camp had recently crossed there. It was growing dark, and rather than take the chances of losing this trail in the night, it was determined to bivouac in the vicinity, rest the animals, and

THE ATTACK ON THE SCOUTS AT DAY-BREAK.

continue the pursuit at the first streak of dawn. It was well that th,s course was decided upon, or there would have been none left to tell the story of the fight, as the result will show. The spot selected for the bivouac had some slight strategic value, and was for that reason chosen by the General, though he had no idea at the time that any benefit would result from his judgment in this particular. It was an elongated low mound of sand (such as are seen at intervals in the Arkansas) which a Fork (Arrickaree) of the Republican at this point embraced as it were (as the Cheyenne does the Black Hills), and formed an island. If this trail had not been struck, it was the intention to have gone back to Wallace for provisions, as only sufficient for one day remained, but upon prospects of a fight it was unanimously agreed to go on and take the chances of something to eat. In the early gray of the next morning while the stars were still twinkling and sleep oppresses more than at any other hour, the sentinels posted on the hills above the island yelled " Indians ! "

In a moment the camp was awake, and with rifle in hand each scout rushed for the lariat to which his horse was picketed, knowing, of course, that the first effort on the part of the Indians would be to stampede the animals. As it was, a small party of the savages dashed in with a horrid whoop, and shaking their buffalo robes, succeeded in running off a portion of the pack-mules, and one or two of the horses.

A few shots fired by the most advanced of the scouts

scattered the Indians, and quiet reigned again for a few moments.

Almost immediately, however, and before the scouts had completed saddling their horses—which the general had ordered—one of the guides nearest Forsyth happening to look up, could not help giving vent to the expression "Great God! General, see the Indians!" Custer, in his Life on the Plains, in referring to this fight says: "Well might he be excited. Over the hills, from the west and north, along the river, on the opposite banks, everywhere, and in every direction they made their appearance. Finely mounted, in full war paint, their long scalp locks braided with eagles' feathers, and with all their paraphernalia of a barbarous war party, with wild and exultant shouts, on they came"

. It was a desperate looking preponderance of brute force and savage subtlety against the coolness and calm judgment of the disciplined soldier; but he, without glancing at the hell in front, and all around him, with only the lines of determination in his face a little more marked, and grasping the terrible picture before him, stoically ordered his men to take possession of the sand mound, with their horses, and then determined, almost against hope, to accept the wager of battle.

It happened, fortunately, that on this island were growing some stunted shrubs, to which the animals were fastened, their bodies forming a cordon, inside of which the luckless scouts prepared for the demoniacal charge which they knew must come with its terrible uncertainty in a few moments.

They had scarcely secured their horses before, like the shock of the whirlwind, on came the savages, and the awfully unequal battle commenced.

It was not yet daylight, and the Indians, taking advantage of the uncertain light, dismounted from their ponies, and creeping to within easy range, poured in a murderous fire upon the scouts.

The Indians were splendidly armed, as usual, by the munificence of the government, or its apathy in preventing renegade white men or traders from supplying them.

When the morning came, which had been anxiously waited for by the scouts, they then first realized their desperate situation.

Apparently as numerous as the sand grains of their little fortification, the Indians hemmed them in on all sides; more than a thousand hideously painted and screaming warriors surrounded them, with all the hatred of the race depicted on their fiendish countenances, in anticipation of the victory which seemed so certain.

Scattered among these, out of rifle range, were the squaws and children of the aggregated bands watching with gloating eyes the progress of the battle, while the hills re-echoed their diabolical death chant and the howling of the medicine-men and chiefs inspiring the young warriors to deeds of daring.

No one can form the slightest conception of the horrid picture spread before the scouts, on the clear gray of that morning, unless he or she has realized it in encounters with the hostile tribes on the Plains. Language is inadequate, and all attempts at word-painting fall so far short of the reality that it were better left wrapped in its terrible incomprehensibleness.

The General and his brave men took in their chances at a glance, but saw little hope in the prospect; they determined, however, never to be taken alive—a thousand deaths by the bullet were preferable to that—and made up their minds to fight to the bitter end, which would only come when the ammunition was exhausted or themselves killed.

To this purpose they commenced to intrench as best they could, by scraping holes in the sand with the only implements at their command—their knives. They succeeded in making a sort of a rifle-pit of their position, but before the work was completed two of the scouts were killed outright and many wounded—among the latter the General himself.

Owing to the dreadful firing of the Indians, who continuously charged down upon the "island," the Doctor was compelled to abandon his care of the wounded and become a combatant; he did excellent work with his rifle, but a bullet soon pierced his brain and he, too, fell over dead.

In a few seconds after the Doctor's death, in the midst of a terrible onset by the Indians, the General was again struck near the ankle, the ball perforating the bone as perfectly as if done with an auger.

The fire of the scouts had not, all this time, been without telling effect upon the Indians—many a painted warrior had bitten the dust before the sun was two hours high. At each successive charge of the red-skins the scouts, cool, careful and deliberate, *took aim*, and when their rifles were dis charged each put a savage *hors du combat*—there was no ammunition wasted.

Nor had the besieged escaped from the fearful onsets of their enemies; besides the casualities related, nearly all the horses had been killed—in fact before noon *all but one had fallen*—and it is related that when he too was killed, one of the warriors exclaimed, "There goes the last d—d horse, anyway."

At this juncture, too, with all their horses killed, and half the number of the scouts either killed or wounded, the Indians determined upon one grand charge which should settle the unequal contest. So they rallied all their forces and hazarded their reputation upon the aggregated assault.

This charging column was composed of some one hundred and fifty "Dog Soldiers" and nearly five hundred more of the Brules, Cheyennes and Arrapahoes, all under the command of the celebrated chief, "Roman Nose."

I quote from Custer again who tells of this charge as it was told to him by the most intelligent of the surviving scouts, and as it has been told dozens of times to the writer : "Superbly mounted, almost naked, although in full war dress, and painted in the most hideous manner, formed with a front of about sixty men, they awaited the signal of their chief to charge, with the greatest confidence."

Their leader at first signaled to the dismounted men beyond his line of horsemen to fire into the scouts, and thus make his contemplated charge more effective. At the moment of the fusillade: "seeing that the little garrison was stunned by the fire of the dismounted Indians, and rightly judging that now, if ever, was the proper time to charge, "Roman Nose" and his band of mounted warriors, with a wild, ringing war-whoop, echoed by the women and children on the hills, started forward."

"On they came, presenting even to the brave men awaiting the charge, a most superb sight.

"Soon they were within the range of the rifles of their friends, and, of course, the dismounted Indians had to slacken their fire for fear of hitting their own warriors.

" This was the opportunity for the scouts.

"Now!" shouted Forsyth, and the scouts, springing to their knees, and casting their eyes coolly along the barrels of their rifles, opened upon the advancing savages a deadly fire.

" Unchecked, undaunted, on dashed the warriors; steadily rang the sharp reports of the frontiersmen. "Roman Nose" falls dead from his horse; "Medicine Man" is killed, and for an instant the column, now within ten feet of the scouts, hesitates—falters.

" A cheer from the scouts, who perceived the effect of their well directed fire, and the Indians begin to break and scatter in every direction, unwilling to rush to a hand to hand struggle.

"A few more shots and the Indians are forced back beyond range.

"Forsyth inquires anxiously, "Can they do better than that, Grover?"

"I have been on the Plains, General, since a boy, and never saw such a charge as that before."

"All right, then, we are good for them."

It was in this grand charge, led in person by their greatest of all warriors, "Roman Nose," that Lieutenant Beecher was mortally wounded. He suffered intensely and lingered some hours before his manly spirit was extinguished.

He and I were warmly attached to each other. I knew "full well" the generous impulses of his warm young heart, and his perfect unselfishness.

He was brave, the very soul of honor and a favorite in all garrisons.

I could not write of his death without interpolating here my simple tribute to his memory. It is a burning shame that such as he are so frequently offered up on the altar of a barbarous policy, dictated by a great Government, that should be *honest enough* with its wards to preclude the possibility of such outbreaks as our so-called Indian wars.

Before night closed in on the terrible tragedy of that day, the Indians charged upon the weary and beleagured scouts again and again, but were as often driven back by the dreadful accuracy of the rifles of the besieged with an increasing loss each time.

The earnestly looked for darkness at last brought the welcome respite, and it was made possible for the unfortunate men to steal a few moments' rest, that was needed—oh! how much!

Hungry, exhausted, with an empty commissariat, every animal dead, four comrades lying stark upon the dreary sand, and a greater number writhing in all the agony of torturing wounds; a relentless enemy ever watching; no skilled hand to alleviate the sufferings of the dying, and the only hope of help that might never come, more than a hundred miles away.

Think of it, grasp it if you can!

Later, while the night yet thickened, preparations were made to meet the events that must surely come with the morning's light, and the little fort, for it now had certainly reached the dignity of that title—was made still stronger; for gabions, the swollen carcasses of the dead horses were used, and huge slices were cut from their thighs for food.

Thank God! the tortures of thirst were not added to their other sufferings, for water was easily obtained by digging a short distance.

Thus strengthened, a midnight council of war was held in whispers, and it was determined to send two of their number to Fort Wallace, as desperate as the undertaking was—and a mere boy—Stillwell and another scout (of whose name

I have no memorandum at hand) expressed their willingness to make the attempt.

The brave men crawled from the "island" to run the gauntlet of the watchful savages ever on the alert to take advantage of the least unfavorable demonstration on the part of their prey, as they fully believed them.

We will leave them making their way cautiously but hopefully in the darkness, for it is not the purpose of the writer at this time to tell of the noble efforts of these brave messengers in their "hair-breadth escapes" on their lonesome and perilous journey.

The details would furnish a separate chapter which may some day be given, but let us turn to the worn out and wounded band of heroes again, and learn how they fared during the long days before help could possibly reach them, even were Stillwell and his companion able to reach Wallace.

The sun rose in all the splendor of a Kansas Autumn morning, but the landscape bore the same horrid features of the day before. All through the weary hours the Indians kept up an incessant firing, but no serious charge was attempted—they had had more than they anticipated in their efforts in that direction yesterday—so the scouts pretty effectually intrenched, suffered but little from the wild firing of their besiegers, but it was annoying, and kept the scouts ever prepared for a possible charge, the result of which might not be so fortunate as that of former ones.

Night again came to throw its mantle of rest upon the little band, and shortly after dark two more scouts were sent out to reach Fort Wallace, if possible, but failed to get beyond the line of watchful savages and were compelled to abandon the idea.

This unsuccessful attempt to go for help cast a gloom over the command, for it could not yet be known what had been the fate of the other two who had gone out the night previously.

The next day the state of affairs assumed a more cheerful aspect—if that could be possible—the squaws and children had disappeared, which indicated a retreat upon the part of the Indians, although they still kept up their firing at intervals—perhaps they too were getting short of ammunition and provisions!

In the afternoon, too, they hoisted a white rag upon a pole and expressed a desire to talk, but our heroes were too wary to be caught with such chaff as that, for with Indians a flag of truce means a massacre half the time.

That night, two more men were sent out, and these carried that famous dispatch of Forsyth's, which should hold its place in history with that other memorable one of Grant's: "I intend to fight it out on this line if it takes all summer.". Forsyth's read:

"I am on a little island, and have still plenty of ammunition left. We are living on mule and horse meat, and are entirely out of rations. If it were not for so many wounded

I would come on and take the chance of whipping them, if attacked. They are evidently sick of their bargain. I can hold out for six days longer, if absolutely necessary, but please lose no time."

The morning of the fourth day, on the now historical little island, broke somewhat more cheerful still; the Indians could be seen rapidly moving away, only a few, comparatively, remaining in sight, to wait until entire exhaustion and starvation should place the scouts in their power—but they little knew the metal of the men lying behind those breastworks of rotten carcasses, or they too, would have gone with the old men women and children of the tribe.

But few shots were fired by the scouts in reponse to the occasional random fusillade of the Indians; they contented themselves with saving their ammunition for a possible last grand act in the drama, and only shooting when an Indian came within certain range, and then he was sure to be sent to the "happy hunting grounds."

Night again came, with its relative rest, and then another weary day of watching and waiting, without any special demonstration on the part of the Indians.

But new horrors made their appearance in the shape of gangrened wounds, and suffering for want of food. The putrid flesh of the dead horses and mules was all that remained that would support life, and however revolting, it had to be swallowed. The nauseating effluvia of the rapidly decaying carcasses too, made the place almost intolerable, and so insufferable did it become that the General told those who were disheartened to go, but all to a man, to their honor be it recorded, refused, electing to remain with their companions in arms—to be rescued, or die with them.

Two more days of torture and then, on the ridge between them and the golden sunlight, gleamed the bright bayonets of Col. Carpenter and his column of "the boys in blue."

Their Havelock had reached this American Lucknow, and cheer after cheer—feeble though they were—went up from the little island, and our story closes with the rescue of these o'er brave men.

A LIVELY RACE WITH THE KIOWAS.

Knowing that my friend, Theodore Sternbergh, Esq., now of St. Louis—son of Rev. L. Sternbergh, D. D., of Ellsworth—sometime in the early settlement of Ellsworth county, had experienced one or two hair-breadth escapes from the Kiowas, who, at that time, under the chieftainship of the dreaded Satanta, hung on the edge of the settlements to gather a few scalps, I desired him to jot down at his leisure, something of the stirring events that had come under his own observation during the time he and I were pleasantly situated as neighbors on the classic Smoky Hill, then a decided Indian country. The result of that request I herewith give our readers, assuring them it is veritable history. My friend writes me:

"You are aware that in the winter of 1870 I had located a homestead in Rice county, covering what is known as the Stone Corral, on the Little Arkansas river. On the evening of the 6th of August, 1870, in company with A. E. Matthews, of Wilson, I started from Ellsworth to visit my place. We obtained a buggy at one of the stables in Ellsworth, and a good-sized, raw-boned, razor-backed, unfortunate livery horse, with Matthews' mare, composed our team. Stopping at Father's place on the Smoky, while Matthews remained in the buggy, I brought out the necessary supplies for the trip. For arms we had a double-barreled shot gun and a revolver each, with plenty of powder and buckshot. We did not anticipate any trouble, but, expecting to be absent several days, we intended to kill some wild turkeys.

"Taking the Fort Sill trail, we drove several miles south of Bradley's Springs and went into camp on the morning of the 7th. As soon as it was light we resumed our journey. The morning was very foggy. As soon as the sun came up and the fog was dispelled so that objects could be readily seen, the country appeared to be alive with antelope and we discharged the shot gun and several loads from the pistols at them, but without killing any. The Fort Sill trail, you remember, after it crosses the large flat south of the Smoky, and approaches the Little Arkansas, passes across the heads of innumerable ravines or gullies, that trend toward that river. This portion of the road is very rough for several miles, but before crossing the eastern fork of that river, the trail is even and good."

"The sun was now fairly up, and we were driving rapidly. While I was very busy attending to my animals, as we approached the east fork, Matthews started up from his seat, saying he saw a herd of buffalo; I replied that I thought this impossible, as I had already been all through the country where we then were the previous week, and felt sure there could be no buffalo anywhere near us. We were now begining to descend toward the bottoms along the east fork. In another moment he said:"

"Those are horses, I see eight of them."

"I replied, if you see horses, there are Indians about; and immediately stopped the team. Looking at the objects he pointed out, I saw there were eight horses, apparently feeding, about half a mile from us. Almost at the same moment the riders—until then unseen—straightened up in their saddles and dashed toward us; Indians, sure enough! The horses scented them, and, turning, began to run. We were nearly twenty miles from the settlements and so determined that our best plan was, to put back for the broken ground, where, perhaps we might place the team in some depression and prevent their being stampeded, while we made the best fight we were able. Matthews took the reins, while I prepared our arms for the expected fight. Placing the pistols on the seat, so as to be handy in case of close quarters, I took the shot gun for the purpose of loading it. I looked some time for the powder flask, but was unable to find it, and asked Matthews where he had placed it. He said '*he* hadn't seen any powder,' and sure enough there was no flask in the buggy. We had no reloads for our pistols, and things began to look slightly bilious. The number of our pursuers had, in some way, been multiplied by two, and they were after us as fast as their ponies could travel. We were not prepared for a fight, even if the odds had not been so great, and our only chance was to run for it, and try to reach the hay camp at Bradley's Springs. While the road was smooth, our team gallantly held their own, and perhaps would have won in time, had the road continued level."

"We soon reached the broken ground, and our horses were fast becoming unmanageable in crossing the gullies. At the bottom of the ravines we could not follow the turns of the road so as to get the safe crossings, but took them straight and on the fly. The Indians now rapidly gained on us, and were hardly a quarter of a mile behind. We could hear their yells—not the most pleasant music in the world to us at that time. Our buggy was liable to be smashed at any moment. There was but one thing for us to do—to leave it and mount our horses. Turning them against the face of a hill steep enough to stop them, we unharnessed our quadrupeds about as quickly as ever that thing was done in Kansas, and sprang upon them, saddleless as they were. I happened to get the razor-back. The Indians were almost upon us, and yelling like a pack of wolves."

"Then ensued a magnificent race—prize, our hair. It was up hill and down; my hat flew off at the first ditch; I did not stop to pick it up, the truth is, it was a little out of fashion. I now have great respect for my livery horse, for he proved to be like a singed cat, better than he looked. For a short time he breathed so hard, that I feared he would fail altogether."

"Matthews's mare ran easily, but soon the horse received somehow a fresh supply of wind, and we ran neck and neck.

We gradually gained on our pursuers, and when about four miles south of Bradley's Springs were nearly a mile ahead, and they gave up the chase."

" We went on to Harker, and with a small escort I returned for the buggy. The vehicle was uninjured, but the Indians had taken every strap of the harness, blankets, picket ropes, etc. Part of our lunch consisted of some of Hon. D. B. Long's cheese; this the Indians had not touched, but all the other eatables had disappeared."

"This race would have been splendid to have witnessed from the grand stand—the time was good, though no record of it was made. My physical feelings were too deeply hurt to appreciate humor just then. I was entirely satisfied with bare back riding, and it grieved me to have my friends insist that I should *sit down* and tell them all about it—I preferred to stand up."

"If you know the Indian who has my shot gun, please tell him chickens are plenty, and I wish he would return it. He may keep the hat. Perhaps I might not inopportunely add that the powder flask was found hanging on the fence at the ranch on the Smoky, just where we had left it."

SE-QUO-YAH.

In only a few instances have the people, in naming the streams, and the more than a hundred counties of the State, perpetuated the legends and the memory of the heroes of the Indian tribes that only a few short years since held almost undisputed possession of Kansas.

The Indian's speech lingers oftener on the rivers and mountains of New England than in the New West—to its shame be it said.

We wish our people would adhere more rigidly to the beautiful sounds of the Sioux, Cheyennes or Arrapahoes—certainly Ta-to-ka is more euphonous than Skunk Creek, or Ta-chanta-wak-pa than Turkey or Dry Creek, and Ninnescah is more poetical than Smithville or Bungtown.

Aside from the mere æsthetics of the idea, with the Indian names are associated the legends, traditions or historic facts of the locality, for the Indian constructs his nomenclature out of actual occurrences on the spot he names, and with the preservation of these primitive appellations by us, veritable history is secured to the state—unimportant and trifling in some instances perhaps—but oftener interesting and worthy of a place in our archives.

Sequoyah county, or as it should be written, Se-Quo-Yah, is named in honor of one of the most remarkable men— Indian though he was—of any age.

This county which lies beyond the one hundreth meridian, in the State of Kansas—that much talked of and written about astronomical line, on which and ulterior to, some meteorologists would have us believe lies a veritable desert, whereon nothing will grow—in fact has a soil whose inherent fertility compares favorably with any on the continent, and which by a system of irrigation—simple and ridiculously inexpensive—inaugurated only last season by one of its first settlers, Hon. C. J. Jones, has produced results that astonished even its energetic projector. By a series of shallow ditches the water is drawn from the Arkansas, which falls nearly ten feet to the mile—the odium which attached, but wrongfully to that region has been dissipated, and farms are eagerly sought for; however, it is not of this I propose to write, but of the celebrated Indian from whom the county takes its name.

The mother of Se-Quo-Yah the blood of whose veins was slightly tinged with English, was a Cherokee, and possessed the characteristic beauty of her race in an eminent degree.

The family, without aspiring to the aristocracy of the tribe, "was prominent and influential, and some of her brothers became members of the council."

In 1768 the mother of Se-Quo-Yah met and married a German peddler, known as George Gist, evidently an ignorant, unimportant tramp of a fellow, whose name would never have come down to history but for the fact that he was the father of Se-Quo-Yah and with that fact, based upon the evidence of the mother of Se-Quo-Yah, George Gist steps down and out, long before hi remarkable son was born, or in the language of Se-Quo-Yah's historian, "gathered together his effects, went the way of all peddlers, and never was heard of more."

The historian,* whom we shall now quote in full, in telling the wonderful story of Se-Quo-Yah says:

"George Gist left behind him in the Cherokee Nation a woman of no common energy, who through a long life was true to him she still believed to be her husband. The deserted mother called her babe 'Se-Quo-Yah' in the poetical language of her race. No truer mother ever lived and cared for her child, whom she reared with the most watchful tenderness. With her own hands she cleared a little field and cultivated it, and carried her babe while she drove up her cows and milked them."

"His early boyhood was laid in the troublous times of the war of the Revolution yet its havoc cast no deeper shadows on the widow's cabin."

"As he grew older he showed a different temper from most Indian children. He lived alone with his mother, and had no old man to teach him the use of the bow, or to indoctrinate him in the religion and morals of an ancient, but perishing people. He would wander alone in the forest, and

---

* Hon. W. A. Phillips, of Salina, Kansas.

showed an early mechanical genius in carving with his knife many objects from pieces of wood. He employed his boyish leisure in building houses in the forest. As he grew older, these mechanical pursuits took a more useful shape. The average native American is taught as a question of self-respect to despise female pursuits. To be made a 'woman' is the greatest degradation of a warrior."

"Se-Quo-Yah first exercised his genius in making an improved kind of milk pans and skimmers for his mother. Then he built her a milk house, with all suitable conveniences, on one of those grand springs that gurgle from the mountains of the old Cherokee Nation. As a climax, he even helped her to milk her cows; and he cleared additions to her fields, and worked them with her. She contrived to get a petty stock of goods, and traded with her countrymen. She taught Se-Quo-Yah to be a good judge of furs. He would go on expeditions with the hunters, and would select such skins as he wanted for his mother before they returned. In his boyish days the buffalo still lingered in the valleys of the Ohio and Tennessee. On the one side the French sought them. On the other were the English and Spaniards. These he visited with small pack horse trains for his mother. For the first hundred years the European Colonies were traders rather than agriculturists. Besides the fur trade, rearing horses and cattle occupied their attention. The Indians east of the Mississippi, and living between the Appalachian Mountains and the Gulf of Mexico, had been agriculturists and fishermen. Buccaneers, pirates, and even the regular navies or merchant ships of Europe, drove the natives from the haunted coast. As they fell back, fur-traders and merchants followed them with professions of regard and extortionate prices. Articles of European manufacture —knives, hatchets, needles, bright cloths, paints, guns and powder—could only be bought with furs.— The Indian mother sighed in her heart for the beautiful things brought by the Europeans. The warrior of the southwest saw with terror the conquering Iroquois, armed with the dreaded 'fire-guns' of the stranger. When the bow was laid aside or handed to the boys of the tribe, the warriors became the abject slaves of the traders. Guns meant gunpowder and lead. These could only come from the white man. His avarice guarded the steps alike to bear meat and beaver skins. Thus the Indian became a wandering hunter, helpless and dependent. These hunters traveled great distances, sometimes with a pack on their backs weighing from thirty to fifty pounds. Until the middle of the eighteenth century horses had not become very common among them, and the old Indian used to laugh at the white man so lazy that he could not walk. A consuming fire was preying upon the vitals of an ancient and simple people. Unscrupulous traders, who boasted that they made a thousand per cent. held them in the most abject thrall. It has been carefully computed that these hunters worked, on an average, for ten cents a day. The power of their old chiefs grew weaker. No longer the old man taught the boys their traditions, morals or religion.

They had ceased to be Pagans without becoming Christians. The wearied hunter had fire-water given him as an excitement to drown the sorrows common to white and red. Slowly the politics, customs, industries, morals, religion and character of the red race were consumed.

In this terrible furnace of avarice the foundations of our early aristocracies were laid. Byrd in his "History of the Dividing Line" tells us that a school of sixty-seven Indian children existed in 1720, and that they could all read and write English; but adds, that the jealousy of the traders and land speculators, who feared it would interfere with their business, caused it to be closed. Alas! the people had encountered the iron nerve of Christianity, without reaping the fruits of its intelligence or mercy.

Silver although occasionally found among the North American Indians, was very rare previous to the European conquest. Afterward, among the commodities offered, were the broad silver pieces of the Spaniards, and the old French and English silver coins. With the most mobile spirit the Indian at once took to them. He used them as he used his shell-beads for money and ornament. Natural artificers were common in all the tribes. The silver was beaten into rings, and broad silver bands for the head. Handsome breastplates were made of it, necklaces, anklets and rings for the toes.

It is not wonderful that Se-Quo-Yah's mechanical genius led him into the highest branch of art known to his people, and that he became their greatest silversmith. His articles of silverware excelled all similar manufactures among his countrymen.

He next conceived the idea of becoming a blacksmith. He visited the shops of white men from time to time. He never asked to be taught the trade—he had eyes in his head, and hands, and when he bought the necessary material and went to work, it is characteristic that his first performance was to make his bellows and his tools; and those who saw them say they were well made.

Se-Quo-Yah was now in comparatively easy circumstances. Besides his cattle, his store, his farm, he was a blacksmith and silversmith. In spite of all that has been alleged about Indian stupidity and barbarity, his countrymen were proud of him. He was in danger of shipwrecking on that fatal sunken reef of American character, popularity. Hospitality is the ornament, and has been the ruin, of the Aborigines. His home, his store or his shop became the resort of his countrymen; there they smoked, talked, and learned to drink together.

After Se-Quo-Yah had grown to man's estate he learned to draw. His sketches, at first crude, at last acquired considerable merit. He had been taught no rules of perspective, but while his perspective differed from that of an European, he did not ignore it like the Chinese. He had now a very comfortable hewed-log residence, well furnished with such articles as were common with the better class of white settlers at that time, many of them, however, made by himself. Before he reached his thirty-fifth year he became addicted to convivial habits to an extent that injured his business, and began to cripple his resources.

Unlike most of his race, however, he did not become wildly excited when under the influence of liquor. Se-Quo-Yah, who never saw his father, and never could utter a word of the German tongue, still carried deep in his nature an odd compound of Indian and German trancendentalism; essentially an Indian in opinion and prejudice, but German in instinct and thought. A little liquor only mellowed him—it thawed away the last remnant of Indian reticence. He talked with his associates upon all the knotty questions of law, art and religion.

Indian Theism and Pantheism were measured against the Gospel, as taught by the land-seeking, fur-buying adventurers. A good class of missionaries had indeed entered the Cherokee Nation; but the shrewd Se-Quo-Yah, and the disciples this stoic taught among his mountains, had just sense enough to weigh the good and the bad together, and strike an impartial balance as the footing up for this new proselyting race. It has been erroneously alleged that Se-Quo-Yah was a believer in, or practiced the old Indian religious rites. Christianity had, indeed, done little more for him than to unsettle the pagan idea—but it had done that.

It was some years after Se-Quo-Yah had learned to present the bottle to his friends before he degenerated into a toper. His natural industry shielded him and would have saved him altogether, but for the vicious hospitality by which he was surrounded. With the acuteness that came of his foreign stock, he learned to buy his liquor by the keg. This species of economy is as dangerous to the red as to the white race. The auditors who flocked to see and hear him were not likely to diminish while the philosopher furnished both the dogmas and the whisky. Long and deep debauches were the consequence. Still it was not in the nature of Se-Quo-Yah to be a wild shouting drunkard.

All the great social questions were closely analyzed by men who were fast becoming insensible to them. When he was too far gone to play the mild sedate philosopher, he began that monotonous singing, whose music carried him back to the days when the shadows of the white man never darkened the forests, and the Indian's canoe alone rippled the tranquil waters.

Should this man thus be lost? He was awakened to his danger by the relative to whom he owed so much. His temper was eminently philosophic. He was as he proved, capable of great effort, and great endurance. By an effort which few red or white men can or do make, he shook off the habit, and his old nerve and old prosperity came back to him. It was during the first few years of this century that he applied to Charles Hicks, a half breed, afterward principal chief of the Nation, to write his English name. Hicks, although educated after a fashion, made a mistake in a very natural projects. In his journey to the west, as well as to Washington, he had an opportunity of examining different languages, of which, as far as lay in his power, he carefully availed himself. His health had been somewhat affected by rheumatism. one of the few inheritances he got from the old fur-peddler of Ebenezer; but the strong spirit was slow to break.

He framed a theory of certain relations in the language of the Indian tribes, and conceived the idea of writing a book on the points of similarity and divergence. Books were to a great extent closed to him; but as of old, when he began his career as a blacksmith by making his bellows, so now he fell back on his own resources. This brave Indian philosopher of ours was not the man to be stopped by obstacles. He procured some articles for the Indian trade he had learned in his boyhood, and putting them and his provisions and camp equipage in an ox-cart, he took a Cherokee boy with him as driver and companion, and started out among the wild Indians of the plain and mountain, on a philological crusade such as the world never saw.

One of the most remarkable features of his experience was the uniform peace and kindness with which his brethren of the prairie received him. They furnished him means, too, to prosecute his inquiries in each tribe or clan.

That they should be more sullen and reticent to white men is not wonderful when we reflect that they have a suspicion that all these pretended inquiries in science and religion have a lurking eye to real estate. Several journeys were made. The task was so vast it might have discouraged him. He started on the longest and last journey. There was among the Cherokees a tradition that part of their nation was in New Mexico, separated from them before the advent of the whites. Se-Quo-Yah knew this, and expected in his rambles to meet them. He had camped on the spurs of the Rocky Mountains, he had threaded the valleys of New Mexico, looked at the adobe villages of the Pueblos, and among that race, was neither Spaniard nor Indian, with swarthy face and unkempt hair. He had occasion to moralize over those who had voluntarily become the slaves of others even meaner than themselves, who spoke a jargon neither Indian nor Spanish, Catholics in name, who ate red pepper pies, gambled like the fashionable frequenters of Baden, and swore like troopers.

It was late in the year 1842 that the wanderer, sick of a fever, worn and weary, halted his ox-cart near San Fernando in Northern Mexico. Fate had willed that his work should die with him. But little of his labor was saved, and that not enough to aid any one to develop his idea. Bad nursing, exposure and lack of proper medical attendance killed him. On the far off Rio Grande he sleeps—the greatest man of his race.

On the pages of American Classics Se-Quo-Yah's name will ever shine. He was even greater than Cadmus, the Phœnician. All honor to those who, imbued with a spirit of the highest emulation, named one of our counties at least after Se-Quo-Yah.

Congress at one time contemplated removing his remains east and erecting a suitable monument over them, but the idea has never been carried out and probably never will be, for if the Father of his Country has nothing in the shape of the enduring marble to commemorate his virtues, how much less may we expect that this poor Indian, though the first to vitalize and preserve the Indian language to history shall be thus remembered! Se-Quo-Yah's monument will ever be the hallowed reverence in the hearts of his people, and that magnificent area of our beautiful prairie whose legal limits bear his name.

WILL THE BUFFALO BECOME EXTINCT?

During Kendall's Santa Fe Expedition in 1841, the party one evening while camping somewhere on the banks of the Arkansas, were visited by an old trapper, and a discussion arose in relation to the immense numbers of buffaloes that were feeding in the bottom a few miles up the river. Kendall asked the old man:

"How many buffaloes did you ever see at one time?"

"Can't say exactly; probably between two and three millions," replied the old man, with a cool matter-of fact indifference, as much as to say, that he was keeping as near the truth as possible.

I do not say that I have seen two or three millions at the same time, but I have stood upon a high roll of the prairie, with neither tree nor brush to obstruct the vision in any direction, and have seen these animals grazing upon the plain and darkening it at every hand. And once I rode with a party of friends in the winter of, 1868 for four days through one continuous herd.

There are perhaps larger herds in Northern Texas than anywhere else on the western prairies, because their most powerful enemies, the Indians, do not range so low down on account of the whites, but every year their numbers are rapidly decreasing, and their range, owing to the encroachment of the settlements from the east and south, becomes more and more circumscribed.

It would seem impossible, especially to any one who has seen them as numerous as the sands on the sea-shore, on their immense natural pastures, that they could ever be extinct, yet when we look back only a decade ago, and remember how even near Pawnee Rock they roamed in such numbers, and now how far off the nearest are, we feel compelled to believe that, like the Dodo and Great Auk, in a few years they will be seen only stuffed, and in a museum.

www.ingramcontent.com/pod-product-compliance
Lightning Source LLC
Chambersburg PA
CBHW031330230426
43670CB00006B/299